...IN THE LAST DAYS OF AMERICA'S HEGEMONY

Telltales & Proofs the US is Waning

Wilfred A. Ruhega

For G. G. MPz

Even LOVE can be a sad illusion.
But what about the bones, the flesh and the blood in us?
They are eternal, making us one in each other's body.
Always remember,
All dad wanted was the best for you.

For Roseneth Barekewe K.
Your love as an eternal lantern, the kindest of hearts
Blessed be you amongst mothers
You are appreciated
Only LOVE!

CONTENTS

Title Page 1

Copyright 2

Dedication 3

Foreword 7

Statement of Category 9

Book Organization and Subs 11

Section One: Exposé, Dilemma 15

Section Two: Reflections 28

Section Three: Telltales 45

Section Four: Seeds of Destruction 94

Section Five: Reading the Past 126

Section Six: Man in his Nature 179

A Note 203

Whilst the rise and downfall of hegemonies of empires can somehow be dated: historians know well enough such knowledge often come too late after something(s) significant to the event has gone too far. Rarely, if any, has people in an empire ever caught themselves in the act of building a 'bully' of a nation – thus stop it. Similarly, never have there been a people who ever saw their empire foundering and henceforth acted to stem the process. Rather, people grow bold and self-assured of the future when it is time they should be worrying. This is a story one can decipher throughout the histories of civilizations – from prehistoric Mesopotamian power-houses to the medieval conquerors of the East including Genghis Khan.

I believe Americans (people of USA) will similarly frown on being told their global order is wilting. They are likely going to receive this analysis with scepticism. Or simply with a sneer and a shrug to satisfy their ego. Few may realise their response (or any other similar condescension) is well known in history. For people in empires rarely know when their imperial days are up. Not even the politicians or the 'drones' as Plato calls them. Why? Because in the heydays of any empire power wielders (the drones) happen to have brainwashed the people and themselves thinking they can choose and seal fate. It is hubris - born out of the illusion of power.

For this treatise I careful made studies of empires that went before the USA and the signatures I learned inform astounding facts. One, that what really build empires are different from what make strong polities. Two, whilst empires are simply and squarely power enterprises, polities are people with shared values, core beliefs and identities that resonate. Three, whilst empires are powers, polities are shared destiny. Four, the strength and determination of the people with feelings of shared destiny, if opportunities arise, build empires (power enterprises). That way comes hegemonies... That is to say, hegemonies are dependent offshoots.

Hegemonies will thus survive as long as polities that found them still hold onto values nourishing common destiny: shared values, core beliefs and identities that resonate. When those values are torn apart or reneged, the strength of the polity is lost. Then facades of power may reveal themselves and machinations conceal a waning civilisation. Yet the fact remains as bright as is a star: that such entity can no longer hold the guard. As you read through this treatise you are going to learn more. And it is going to reveal to you *how* the USA has succumbed to forces and philosophical leanings that cause social dislocations and power disintegrations that are preludes to waning.

Welcome.

....

twitter: @WRuhega
facebook: Alexinho Ruhega

BOOK ORGANIZATION AND SUBS

Section One: Exposé, Dilemma

Part One
Subs: America Discovers Being Trapped
       Allies, Suckers

Part Two
Subs: Sloppy Economic Intelligence, Diplomacy
         Europe, China: Investing in America's
       Preoccupation

Section Two: Reflections

Part Three
Subs: The Dawn of America's Global Leadership
         America in the Shoes of an Executioner

Part Four
Subs: A Military that is an Investment
         Americans: Hostages of Military Complexes

Part Five
Subs: America's Reins of Power–Who Pulls Them?
         Overlooking has a Price
         Internal Rifts and their Allied Emergencies

Section Three: Telltales

Part Six
Subs: A Cunning Military Complex Ever Seen
         Can Americans Decide their Fate?

Part Seven
Subs: The Money and Politics of this Superpower
         The Liability the US Intelligence is
         A Fact: Civilizations Were Here Before
       the USA

Part Eight
Subs: The Falcon Cannot Hear the Falconer
         Sheer Uncertainty
         Drudgery is the Word

Part Nine

Subs: A Treacherous Economy

America's Imperialism, Curse of Patriotism

The Centre Cannot Hold

Part Ten

Subs: The US Democracy is a Phantom

US Democratic Practice in the Eyes of Plato

America Outdoing Herself

Section Four: Seeds of Destruction

Part Eleven

Subs: The True Maker of America's Greatness is   Woodrow Wilson

The Rejected, Shredded Dreamer Won in Death

Woodrow's Democracy Re-considered

America's Democracy is a Dracula

Core Values under Attack

Part Twelve

Subs: Lo Narrates

The Narratives and the Reality about Mankind

Modern Civilizations Following Old Paths

Humanity is Elusive

America in the Footprints of Ancient Rome

Part Thirteen

Subs: Rome is Gone

Rome's Pallbearers

Is the US Faring Better?

Section Five: Reading the Past

Part Fourteen

Sub: Before Rome Eased Down Hill

Part Fifteen

Subs: Civilization are a Continuum

From Old Rome to Washington

The Great Gathering

Americans Belong to the God YAHWEH

Rome – Reconfigured
The Repeat: Mistakes of Rome, Greece
Part Sixteen
Subs: Covet and Hate at a Go
An Old Wisdom
Part Seventeen
Subs: The Argead Dynasty of Macedonia
The Wars of Alexander the Great
Naturally, Humanly
Plato's Analysis: The Human Numbers
Part Eighteen
Subs: The Middle East, Graveyards of World Empires
Cyrus II and the History of Power
Part Nineteen
Subs: In Persia Long Time Ago
Muslims: Meet Dhul al-Qarynayn
Still there was 'the fall'
The Root

Section Six: Man in His Nature

Part Twenty
Subs: Mankind is Dangerous
The Root of America's Decline
Overlooked in the Art of Empire Building
There 'Has Been'
Part Twenty One
Subs: The Last Throes
Come to America, Come to Europe
Greatness has Great Price
One Time in Egypt
Power Enterprises are dethroned
by Weak, Innocent Civilities
It is not safe to be Alone
A Bank of Stubbornness

SECTION ONE: EXPOSÉ, DILEMMA

...in the Last Days of America's Hegemony (1)

It's written all over the stars that the 'jack of all trades is master of none'. This ages old figure of speech towers high in the clouds. It means 'whoever partakes many skills at a go miss proper knowledge to master even one of them'. As far as I know the weight of this claim hasn't proven insignificant. It still holds.

Over the ages mankind has recorded, the fact one cannot be sage in everything has had manifests either at individual, group or community level. People who don't acknowledge this hold onto hubris only to end 'irrevocable failures'. So are humans, so are nations.

Nations are territorial entities made up of a collection of people. Thus it goes without saying how 'nations replicate aggregate human hearts and minds co-existing'. Nations are polities made of a mass of people and therefore they collectively encounter the wisdom they cannot be jacks of all trades. They are but a sea of humanity. Thus *victims* of humanism they remain. If a nation tries to be the jack of all maybe because she has vast machineries of intellect, intelligence, wherewithal and think-tanks of personnel the fate is the same. Such a nation end up master of none.

In our time the United States of America (US of A) is a reminder to this sage. America is *presently* at a point in time an imperial power try all tricks there are to rule over her dominions. Or simply try to oversee everything civilizations. Hubris. She is the global jack of all trades. But is she mastering any? It would seem not. The sage is holding fast. Here you go...

America Discovers Being Trapped

For outsiders who careful study, analyse and internal watchers who have been students of the comings and goings –

millions of critical Americans included – one 'elusive' fact in the last sixty years has been the indefinable marriage between the USA and majority European mega economies: Britain, Germany, France, Italy, Spain, Belgium and the Nordic countries. Pinpointing the nature of the bond evident amongst those nations has been mystifying, so…

Some analysts see the relationship as an 'alliance'. Within this *reflection* millions of people believe there is 'America and her allies'. That they are fated together by a resonating guileful sort of friendship. To verify global interventions that are 'mind wrenching' to explain, contenders in this school of thought hold that Iraq, Afghanistan and Libya were invaded by the USA and her allies. Or that the 'NATO allies' bombed Slobodan Milosevic. They use this on any other mentioning of the likes. This group I call 'neutered' contenders…

Majority third world commentators (politicians, scholars, academics etc.) name the relationship 'racist'. People in this group – mostly Arabs, Africans and non-whites of Asia – see the USA and Europe essentially as one and the same Caucasian people. Grouping them in the name 'Western Countries' these observers designate the cooperation as a 'sisterhood'. This perceived sisterhood they condemn as racist manoeuvres of the Whites' powers on 'nations-other'. To them the Westerners' closeness is roughly thought of as teaming up of the people of one race against the rest. The West against the rest of us. This group I call 'sceptic' contenders.

The last 'view' on the foregoing has remained materialistic and oftentimes more or less Marxist. With the advent of monopoly capitalism plus its subsequent processes of globalizing, the seemingly unquestionable support European nations accord the USA – in the last sixty years especially – is inferred as 'a monopolistic solidarity'. Majority in this group have had simplistic answers. For example, that developed economies naturally cooperate to monopolise global resources. They put in that America acts class 'head prefect' of monopoly agendas whereas nations in Europe and Canada cherish their class membership.

This group I call 'a poor man's view' contenders.

However convincing the last recourse (the poor man's view) sounds, it has partly been disproven. No one else but the US President Donald J. Trump is to be credited the proofs. How so contrary things turn up, uh! At least logic hunters can *now* sit up and think things over.

Thanks president Trump we are enlightened a bit. So far one can see the traps America is in. The president's precarious position, his frustrations although he is the legal occupier of the White House, his approach to pre-existing issues and resulting 'reactions' from Americans generally have given clues to how America is going to get dethroned of her hegemony. *Tell-tales* are flashing red neon.

The US president has so far revealed that for the last couple of decades European nations and Canada have unbeknownst to many US economists played roles of 'pushcarts' and 'I am-push-me-around' because they are stealthily enjoying America's economy. He is showing that through resounding trade deficits and megalomaniac market imbalance unprecedented in world history, the allies have after all been the smartest. So Trump's America is discovering that the USA has been fighting wars, reaping world resources and mechanising exploitation of global 'valuables' for the benefits of Europe and the wising Chinese corporations. This is the kernel: America has spread military tentacles abroad leaving Europe and China to take sharp fangs onto her internal market.

America turns out to be the loser. And it is clear enough. It's *man in his nature*.

Allies, Suckers

If a keen economist would rationalise in light of the new evidences coming in, he would describe the relationship between Europe and America 'parasitic'. That while the USA is trying to be everything and master anything, she has been and still is in the end, earning for the whole West. The world of business is overly tricky. China and *some* headstrong industrial economies are equally dipping in the same bowl of soup. Now there is this story of a very smart US economy that is suffering towering trade deficits against allies and competitive economies. Sky high trade deficits mean the lion's share of what America's corporate society earns abroad *soon* get rat-holed to Europe, Canada, China etc.

Gradually, almost imperceptibly, the USA is becoming an emporium *than* the first rate hegemon she boasts of. This is the likeness of how elusive this world is. Many empires gone before the US suffered similar breakdown.

Of all one can accuse the yelping Donald Trump, what he is going about rectifying and reviewing America's traditional exposure to the world of fellow competitors is not without density. He is somehow justified – he is trying to see beyond the obvious. An interesting observation though is that some '*know-all*' American economists are not yet coming to terms with the fact. They cannot help themselves to the fact the president has acted smarter and is exuding better economic intelligence than they have been. It is in the character of many economists, especially when they think they are indispensable.

Donald Trump's stance on redoing trade agreements are in effect admission that the wars they have been fighting together – with Europe putting in few millions of dollars in cash and materials – have served 'covers' for the allies to steal America at geometric progression. The millions put in by 'friends' are pennies deducted off gigantic income Europe scoops through 'a rat hole' of trades. That is what the president is finding out – and he is possibly right. After all he is a brilliant businessman. He might have sharper eyes than a horde of bookworm economists.

But how did all that schism start?

It started when America, through the blood of millions spilled in the 1st and 2nd world wars, chose to be the West's 'jack of all trades...' Yet this is a tip of an iceberg. It is a clear indicator of a crumbling hegemony yes, yet by no means the better of other *tell-tales*.

This treatise takes you further – to grander *'seeds of destruction'*. Seeds and tell-tales by which you are going to see the US doing an unmistakable imperial manoeuvres of a dying head of civilization...

And there is history to attest to all those manoeuvres and their lived impact. How and when the impact germinate to bring forth a fruit that is death of empires is lucidly pinpointed. All one has to do is *"Reading the Past"*.

This is an open secret: the USA is the most staffed when it comes to security operatives, intelligence and war support technologies. Her Intel alone is so vast and robust a machinery it chugs millions of dollars each day.

The US has her intelligence gathering far flung, mechanically crafted and wide spread that *officers* crawl all over the world. They analyse and profile other nations' policies, politicians, laws, businesses, security and they do any other snort business. Poking her nose in other countries' affairs is America's primary strength; however, that is her eventual weakness. For it is true that a man's strength is his weakness. With her curiosity for unleashed presence everywhere and in anything, she has for the last 100 years been the jack of all trades. This far she espouses 'a hypothetical' illusion she can coach the universe.

The USA is in each country's matters. From human rights to trade in weapons, internal policies to marketization and so forth. This pervasiveness is *in the end* responsible for blinding her of the most natural things. Some of them being; that of being careful of friends and remaining true to oneself. Most empires now lying in ashes would tell fuller stories about this blindness. Sadly they cannot have a second chance.

Note that the present US hegemony first rose as a military power. Say, a military intelligence. That is, a polity whose military operations are buoyed and turned on by outputs of smooth intelligence gathering. She would later become the economic stays of the West *particularly* after deciding World War I and II. It was decline of Europe following adverse effects of the major wars that the *un*destroyed US took lead. America was lucky, not mighty. *Luck* is known to decide a lot in ways more than one. And yet it cannot be overstretched. None is ever lucky to be forever lucky.

Sloppy Economic Intelligence, Diplomacy

Life as head prefect (a hegemon) brings to the USA many exploits doled out to unquenchable ambitions. Policies she adapts bespeak arrogance – especially those that authorises intervening in other nations' affairs. Her robust intelligence becomes 'a base' for dictating global economy, politics, agitation and a *host* of underhanded manoeuvres. This, whilst *all* possible and palatable within planning phases – in Washington to say – they are catastrophic in executing phases (then outside USA). And they tend to backfire when in actions. Why? Because plans implementation processes out there lose originality. Outside USA, implementers are *on their own* and have to rely on massive 'improvising' as then the world becomes alive and it isn't what framers had in mind. What complexity the sea of humanity is becomes evident... *probably* the reason many wars the USA is making outside are ending in mess of lawlessness. One cannot rule out possibility that *perhaps* the US Army does make twists on prior tactics to arrive to 'other developments' which eventually confuse politicians and the public, who knows? The army's intelligence is after all too sophisticated and as you will learn in due course, it isn't a defence force – and it isn't a machinery for the people. It is for 'America's interests'. Yet majority of those interests never reach the hands of the people.

Anyway, whatever the case is we can glean some informative facts from the recent Iraq Report. The Report details a lot on the US army's exploits in the years following the Iraq invasion and it doesn't paste a rosy picture. It says things are not what they seem.

On the occasion of discussing "The U.S. Army in the Iraq War (the Iraq Report)", Gen. Mark A. Milley, the 39th Chief of Staff, U.S. Army, had this noteworthy things penned on paper,

> *"the OIF is a sober reminder that technological advantages and standoff weapons alone cannot render a deci-*

sion," he continues in more specific terms *"The promise of short wars is often elusive; that the ends, ways, and means must be in balance; that our Army must understand the type of war we are engaged with in order to adapt as necessary; that decisions in war occur on the ground in the mud and dirt; and that timeless factors such as human agency, chance, and an enemy's conviction, all shape a war's outcome."*

In clearer terms, the General is noting how sloppy prior war intelligence is. However detailed an invasion intelligence is made, yet, on the ground the military contingents meet another world – the poor *bastards* they visualised in their imagination aren't what they looked. They are complex, savvy and explosive. The winning tricks must, as Gen. Milley notes, come from "factors such as human agency, *chance*, and an enemy's conviction". But the putter here is not the Pentagon any longer, hear the Gen. say again "that decisions in war occur on the ground in the mud and dirt".

Now there the problem is – chance, in the mud and dirt! Gen. Milley is right. But he could add this; 'the ground with mud and dirt' is in any invasion the defendants' turf – the latter know well their land, they *mostly* prepare it in advance and can connect to the timeless realities quicker than Washington boys can ever do in a short time… And chance isn't a preserve of the US Army anyway.

And so we see Libya, Iraq, Syria, Afghanistan and Yemen degenerating into lawlessness – wars becoming almost unconquerable. Falling in anarchy despite the primary invasions having been results of America's 'good intelligence' and 'thorough military planning'. Results of informed strategizing plus long time tactical crafts they were.

It is always hard. Hard even for the mighty US Army. Can't be easy when 'chance' is one of the determinants. And this explains why the same adept US Army is, twenty years later, going back to Afghanistan hands extended, to beg for peace from and talk to the ragtag Taleban. The latter's human agency has proven indefatigable. And the knowledge they have of their people, timeless factors and chance have proven solid. The same applies to Iraq, Somalia etc.

It would seem that since the USA won global headship by acting 'decider' in the last major wars, she has affinities to violence and arm-twisting. She also reverts to public brainwashing as a means to reach many ends. It is evident America reveres violence. America worships attrition. Washington is the bastion of a modern goddess of war. Her heroes (the likes of Sen. John McCain and general Jim Mattis) are warmongers. Jim Mattis for example has beautiful nicknames: "chaos', 'warrior monk' and 'mad dog'' all from perceived brilliant military exploits.

Actually, the US trusted heroes must have records (ones they parade as proofs of statesmanship/patriotism) of warring. These are for the reason that she is almost always executing strategic wars in various geographical zones, for the last 80 years. Some public figures – Jimmy Carter for example – would prove me wrong. According to ex-president Carter, the US has been at peace only sixteen years of her total 242 years as a nation. He notes that the US is "Most warlike nation in the history of the world". Yeah, I would agree. Some argue Old Rome preceded the US in that respect - I say no. Rome was not a nation state. It was long before the rise of what we now call *nations'*.

America's philosophy that has held steadfastly is: if she cannot win diplomatic feats, she finds ways to make her victims 'failed states'. Or she unleashes internal socio-economic and political dysfunctions in that *poor* country. So... 'they build their world in great confusion to force on others the devil's illusion...' sings Bob Marley in his scathing hit *"ride natty ride"*. You are going to learn more about this song's message.

A salient feature: the USA is essentially formless in matters of relationship. No country can be the US's best of friends, no. Even when such country is a stooge. No. No. No. Once global alignments of power and resources change the US policies methodically change. And this without warning her citizens either. An interpretation of this is that the US 'prefect-hood' is ultra-reactive. Ultra-sensitive. Multifaceted. Versatile. It is not owned and cannot be granted by the people. 'The people' meaning the US citizens. Well? This is a travesty. A danger. A dagger on the-stars-and-stripes. *Read history.* This kind of politicking (is called machtpolitik) is destructive of civilizations. The world has records to attest to it from around the 7th century Before Christ.

The aforesaid 'spanking' destroy civilizations in the sense that imperial states cease to be nations on their own. Or to possess clean conscience of their powers… rather becoming prone to prevailing events.

Put in simple words: the imperial state arrives at a stage in which she mostly reacts to events developing elsewhere. This instead of dealing with her own people-centred issues. And the spirit of a hegemon's decision making machinery at this time sways like a flag in the wind. For example if China decides to adjust (say devalue) her currency, it strains (and becomes headache to) the Washington. If Russia sets a new military base in the Arctic that becomes America's panic. Any UN resolution against Israel's *colonial* Zionism on Palestine becomes America's business. Again, when Ecuador proffers a motion at a UN session for reduced use of 'formula products' by lactating mothers America throws tantrums. See!? If the US was a human being, she surely would die of heart attack. Or she would, at least, succumb to some mental illnesses.

At the end of the day, you find out Americans are left with 'state machineries' extremely outward oriented. Machineries that are working to grapple with the world more than they *stir* Americans. This is a bypassing. In all accounts it is. It is a go-around that reneges the fact that truer safety and integrity come from within – less from without.

Europe, China Investing In America's Preoccupations

That America's eyes are set to envision imperialistic than

popular-driven motives is as clear as is day time. Yet learned in history is, that is a firm ground fertile for self-defeat. The vast wealth the US accumulates outside through her Multinational Corporations (MNCs) is brought home yes. But the impact (almost always overlooked in strong empires) is to turn in billions of money wholly owned by privateers. Not for States or Federal coffers – the two only get taxes from the proprietors. And even at such, they can only collect the tax privateers have decided not to evade.

Thus in practice Americans have a nation wherein some corporate entities/citizens are filthily rich while authorities and 'the people' *only* witness the marvels of being in a country super-rich. Citizens who need bread must toil for the MNCs. The people's services to MNCs convert into a huge secure market. This is because private franchises create multivariate household expenditures and a people constantly in hunger of disposable assets. This fact brings opportunities... Opportunities of immense proportion.

In the case of USA such tempting opportunities have the other, external industrial powers, racketing for expansionism. The ensuing US market sets the rest of us watering our mouth. Those able have crawled under the skin of the 'head Prefect' to suck that juicy market – through trade imbalances. Here is when it turns out that 'a clever bird is caught with chaff'.

America has, inadvertently, turned herself into the most stable and reliable emporium. She now is a centre of tussling 'market forces'. Clever yes, still a colony of trades she is. A spot for battling businesses. No battleground is a fine place.

As noted earlier, America's intelligence cohorts are focused elsewhere, running shows. Outside they are scratching. Leaving ajar the back door. Americans are thus becoming ever expendable. Well, it isn't always smart to be smart. America is proving this point. And this is how trade deficits Donald Trump is cracking over came to soar higher... China, Europe and other global competitors allow the USA to play smart. But they use that preoccupation to bring mountains of (inflated) luxurious wares to the States. See!? The mounting deficits were gradually set in motion. Donald Trump or anyone else is never going to reverse them... Never.

By the way, while Donald can dare take some steps, others are sleepless to stop him. For they have had foreign businesses much wormed in America and are settled very deep in the fabric of the US economy.

Many seasoned politicos know well no way can America backtrack without causing serious economic crashes. Distresses sure to lead America downhill. America needed globalising – because she kind of thought she would play the master. Well, the world has brought globalism to Washington – a rapid response to the famous 'Washington Consensus' schemed in 1980s. Yet it isn't what school textbooks said it would be. One should remind that, 'all masters of games succumb to their own records'.

SECTION TWO: **REFLECTIONS**

The Dawn Of America's Global Leadership

As a proven tradition: a well rooted progress is built upon a well-defined, motion philosophy. A definite framework of thought is usually a primer for sustainability.

Put in clearer words one could say, 'each successful headway advance is based on clearer construction of mind-set'. For example, a smart businessman who eventually succeeds must have had meticulous planning before taking on any meaningful move. One must have sat down to comprehend and devise the details of his trade beforehand. Likewise, a good musician must have had, in his thoughts, early conscience of the messages he wanted delivered. This before he started fingering each commendable song. This is per the law of averages.

The law here presupposes that a primus in any trade is a 'doable' direction of thought. That remains true for people as individuals and for nations as 'communities'. This reality was applicable to the ascent of USA as a hegemon. Someone (*some people*) had to sit down and transform some mundane thoughts previously known as "the *manifest destiny*" that had been recycling in the New World since 1830s. The ideas had to form into an outlook of sharp, unidirectional ambitions. The US imperial power, actions, policies and position on global affairs started, thus, from a clear direction of thought dating back to 1917. That is, starting when she decided to do away with full '*isolationism*'. This start aimed at taking a prominent role in global affairs. Since then 'the world for America' set on the road to Emmaus.

The 1917 'road walk to grab the earth' was an augmenting

adaptation credited to a Woodrow Wilson – the 28th president of USA who justified America's entry into World War I. In his famous words: "the world must be made safe for democracy". So simple and clear the words sounded yet so murky and pretentious they really play out. First, they purport to export an assortment of liberal values to the world. Ask, whose liberal values? Well, America's democratic values they are. Direct transliteration of that is: 'Americanisation of the world'. That is it. Second, the decision became a precedent that gave America courage she could turn the world into what she wanted. It was an advertent fulfilment of the famed manifest destiny. The manifest was a collection of *imperial views* majority US politicians had for decades shied away from. But there they had come, Woodrow Wilson and his contemporaries had found an opportune moment to land them. Well? The Great War had brought possibility.

Isn't it after all said, 'wars build empires?'

Third, the decision to march US democracy on the world spewed a sacrosanct idealism amongst America's top classes. The false idealism that what could work amongst Americans could as well work for the world. The end result of all that is deducible in Lord Collin Renfrew's 'down the line' model (more on this in the last part of this treatise).

The impact of Wilsonian ideas (or whatever they soon plummeted into) in practice became that 'nations-other have to follow America's route', i.e. leading their lives like Americans do. Like: viewing life through Americans' eyelids. Dreaming America's dreams. And having world wide 'dames' look like damsels in New York. It couldn't end up there certainly. It would produce another insulation: that America should cater to her needs by perching her domestic demands (homeland inadequacies actually) on the shoulders of outsiders. This last is the core of her current imperial outlooks – especially her constant attempt to forge (to guide and to reshape) the world into what American entrepreneurs want. To do this right she found out she must become the 'jack of all trades....

America In The Shoes Of An Executioner

It has come to pass that despite the frayed views America had to make of the world – since the time she entered the First World War – she was lucky to emerge the supremo. It was luck not might that saw her out. The ensuing taste of power gave high confidence to her elites and subsequently her policy framers. America's economy had remained the most outstanding in a world that stood in shambles then, and she therefrom achieved yet another feat – one of becoming the financial exchequer and material sponsor of the 'allied' warriors. This is where hails the 'neutered' contenders' view. With the allies in her armpits it was onwards possible to orchestrate moves the USA could use to forge the world into what she wanted. After all, nothing resists money. Money makes men. Money brings honour. And the US had the chunk the world needed. Money was being sought after for reconstruction of the West and all that there was to do. This gives birth to the 'poor man's view' contenders. Money is a god in its own right. Its godhead brings layers of idealisations. The well *known* rows of thought born in this period are named (in the studies of international relations) 'Wilsonianism'. There are many ideas in this school. Wilsonianism is a mother to a doctrine so ambitious and preposterous... The 'Idealist perspective of international relations'.

To remain alive, imperial powers need to be expressed – this in multiple forms. America knew this before 1917 and was hungry to play it. She immediately started restructuring Europe. Candidly speaking, she annexed European 'states' to her policy orientations, economic adjustments (structural frameworks) and influenced their military reorganisations. America had the trump-seed, the money and power to command, and played her game well.

Countries in Europe were in tatters between 1915 and 1945 (*roughly*: interwar period) and had no ability to reassert their pride until two decades after the Second World War. All that whilst they were lingering in the effects of devastating wars. Americanisation took majestic paces and built an unobstructed realm. The more accepting of America's liberalism (and new freedoms as Woodrow had called them) a nation was willing to go, the more American friendship she earned. This gives birth to the 'sceptic view contenders'. For example the UK, having been an immediate coloniser of majority US states and a wholeheartedly adopter of America's liberal mechanisms, rank friendliest of nations. In the words of President George W. Bush "America has no truer friend than Great Britain". Details on how the once fierce, competitive, stoic, proud and independent Britons ever came to be 'minions' of the USA should take several PhDs to pen down.

To date the UK doesn't question what the US does – mostly. There are those rare times Londoners oppose politicians on America's hatched issues – for example fighting unpopular foreign wars at America's beck and call. The Downing Street politicians do scarcely say no to Washington. On some issues they'd rather remain mute. They have made many an unsuspecting mass believe the USA is a better ally than Europe combined. That the US is the UK's sun god. I opine: 'this is where (at least partially) hinged the confidence for Brexit. President Obama alluded to this when he visited Britain, April 2016, shortly before the vote. He cautioned the British that being in the Euro (as an economic block) was safer than leaving and negotiating a deal with US alone. He warned "the UK is going to be in the back of the queue" to get a trade agreement done.

Again the latch for Britain not adopting the Euro coin is *possibly* the arrogance of being closer to the US $. On this, I leave better reasons to prove me wrong.

If one goes to more trouble, examining further – in theory and in practice – one finds out Europe is this far subsumed in America's imperial traditions. But America's imperial traditions (the mires Europeans are stuck in) are geared towards exporting her internal demands to trap other nations' abilities, geographies and resources to America's ambitions. This is central to Wilsonianism. That 'America wills, the world provides'. And this is rooted in a *precocious* belief that 'there is a world for America and an America for Americans'. Yet practical circumstances have it otherwise – this you are going to find out as you read through this treatise.

When in the year 1917 Wilsonian conspiracy was launched, the rest of the world was made up of 'rumbling colonies' of Europe. Therefore 'nations-other' fell to Wilsonianism *by extension*. This way America easily became a global executioner... now the holder of an imperial scythe.

*...in the Last Days of
America's Hegemony (4)*

Any economic historian worthy her salt would tell that America's economic policies conceived during and after the great world wars per Wilsonian 'Machiavellianism' were poisoned.

There is a scholarly argument that idealist policies contain seeds of their own destruction. However clever America's policy framers and economic projectors were (are) ready to go, the world remains exceedingly valiant and perpetually against a single nation's chauvinism. This is a knowledge most empires came to realise at one time or the other. It is remarkable the US empire hasn't crashed this far – at a hundred years old.

In the preceding parts I have so far noted that: first, the trouble with America's imperial mind-set is preoccupation with material wiles than the fate of her people. It is evident not only in rhetoric by America's politicians but also in her military behaviours that are hell-bent she forgets the primary purpose of an army is 'defence' – that, more than anything else. The character of the US army is perverted, so to speak. It considers its might as yet another pillar for political assertion – hence, it is a political Army. This behaviour precludes the US Army from being a machinery for people's defence *mainly* but one for strategic offensives.

Second, there is this astounding fact: statistics by States and Federal government show that America's social sectors: roads, public health, railways, public schools and welfare mechanisms in decrepit conditions. This is public abandonment, if only to speak. It has been a cry for decades. Remember part of the waves that washed Donald Trump to the Oval office in 2016 were promises to revamp those social sectors. He told cheering crowds of supporters, again and again, he would rehabilitate roads and other social infrastructures that are dying *not* to send money (aids and loans) to foreign nations - fighting wars in countries he later would call "shitholes". Revisit Trump's campaign promises you will hear that. He sounds categorically firm.

Also remember (you can easily double check online) those very promises were there in Obama's roseate speeches (many of them before getting elected). You can quote me: later candidates will be promising the same – twenty years plus from now. The reason is clear, read on...

Stand out now to reflect: what is and what is not America's eminence? Doesn't it seem that the preeminence perceived of America (by outsiders) lack corresponding internal solid, sustainable welfare structures? It is your call to make decision.

And think this: America is the biggest global debtor.

Reason this: where do the billions they earn go?

Those questions lead us to the third reflection. That of the role of America's military being a money mine, a treacherous investment. This viewed against global, historical traditions and the rationale of *soldiering*. This third reflection is critical towards understanding this treatise. Be open, be dynamic. Many will 'herein and about' remain unsaid yet much intended. That is, very implied.

A Military That Is An Investment

Think critically: Statistics show – this is evident if you flip the Pentagon's own budget in the last five years – America's expenditure and investment in the army keep looming as per yearly receipts. This is led by the Ministry of Defence's cheque books. Overall lion's share of budgetary increment is led by what is piled upon previous years' military expenditure on arsenals (often). Interpreted: this means America keeps, principally, invigorating her weaponry and military stockpiles. That is; warplanes, tanks, artilleries, warheads, drones, bullets and the air strikes technical facets take more than what the people receive. And they are the taxpayers to that end. And they are a bit over 328 million heads. A glaring misplacement of resources, wouldn't you say? Perhaps you should. Depends on your conscience though!

Along the submissions made so far add *an eye opener* that preferred expenditure on the military attracts pervasive propensity to do violence. This is the fourth of the facts thereof. America heavily invests in her military complex in order to use it satisfactorily. Say, the deciders do not mean it for a waste. It is an investment. An investment is *presumably* a capital launch used on an assumption that profiting it will do. Now think the gravity of this assumption. What happens when a military becomes an investment?!

The military, however sophisticated and adept it is, is there to use force – no sugar-coating is required here. An army is a bloodletting machine through the use of force. But force sleeps at Mrs Violence's homestead. When no physical violence is made, at least threats of it are in stock. See? Herein lies the reason America, as she is today, cannot guard agreements for peace (i.e commitment to peace treaties/accords) with any country – not Iran, Russia, North Korea, China or any other docile state.

Jong-Un accuses America of "not working issues in good faith". Think he got it right, but had seen it myopically.

Tell Jong-Un the fact is 'without an atmosphere of violence and some strategic travesties, America's military complex *now* guzzling billions of taxpayers' dollars a month would be a waste'. Washington isn't foolish to get to that point. Frankly speaking no empire in history has ever afforded that 'throw-money-around'.

Again, some clever Washington fellows sitting on the shoulders of power-brokers wouldn't have the excuses they put forward to press for more money come each year's budget.

In the mind-set of hegemons, 'the world must be set on hot, steaming plates'. That way they can keep their imperial armies profitable.

Americans: Hostages Of Military Complexes

Choose to delimit the concept 'military complex'. Let us extend its reference to spy agencies, field forces of all categories, security operatives and the regular armies – the green berets, the naval and the Air Force. Again, incorporate the weaponry departments and their allied facilities/installations in the same delimitation. If you analyse the felt impact of all those forces to the US life story, you realise that what the 'squeaky' politicians at the Capitol debate are offshoots of manoeuvres the military complexes hatch. It is evident spy agencies are autonomous. And that they have hijacked prominent civil powers of States and Federal nature. For example, it is alleged by some that on getting early tips the Pentagon and WTC could be blown (the 9/11 incidence) the spy agencies took their time. With that laxity, thousands got blown on the spot and others were wasted in the misguided planes. Billions of dollars' worth of properties were razed down. The twin towers got lamentably destroyed. There, you see, was a show of violence.

That happened, so analysts argue, that the public could be leashed and made to accept myriads of security and Intel expenditures. This game plan is 'preying on people's fear'.

Further down that line of manoeuvres: media and spy reports reveal that some super-at-lying elements amongst security agencies had fabricated rumours of Saddam Hussein's arsenal of chemical weapons. That it was the Bush administration's ruse. To serve what end? Think it over again. Some argue that the trick was to unseat Saddam. If you look further in that incidence, you realise how military ploys – not people's power or the commoners' votes as American simpletons boast – do shape the determinants of the US foreign policies.

The agencies have the reins that pull together some excuses for actions, routes to prepare policy environment and subsequently propose tentative ways forward. This achievement is a culmination of many years of *psy-ops* that have perfected clandestine means of decision management. The public is thus cheated of its dimes. Cheated of its times. Cheated of its votes. Cheated of its dreams. Others are more than meets the eyes.

See!? Even the American President – Donald Trump today in 2020 – is crying foul play as a result of that practice. He is constantly 'yelping' that 'engineered' fake news or intelligence leaks are trying to take him down. He thus is changing his military and security advisers (personnel) at an alarming rate.

In Moscow one time (that was besides the Capitol's own nightmare, president Vladimir Putin) Trump rejected his spy agencies' allegations he had colluded with Russia to steal elections. He called it a *witch-hunt*. A fabrication. So far events have proven Trump right. For no legal course has been pursued against him to prove his culpability in defrauding the American voters. One would judiciously agree that there is an issue of credibility in the security agencies... an issue that *sadly* doesn't go away. Or so history proves...

America's Reins Of Power – Who Pulls Them?

When a nation arrives at a point in time the first citizen – the President, the King – is equally worried of credibility of his intelligence agencies something is grossly wrong. At that point, the agencies have become way socially irrelevant. And they rather are tools of manoeuvres.

The US has of late become close to this. Her vast spy body is resolutely engaging politicians – the president mostly – to keep them on edge. A very far reaching mistake that is.

From the histories of power learned is that when politicians are set on edge by those who should protect them, they fall prone to manipulations. And consequently do behave as mad as a March hare. The US Intel brasses seem to have scored an A in this lesson. They are baiting their fishes and are missing not a bite. They have some fat sizzling on 'la Cornue's Grand Palais range' and the fishes can't swim in hot fat. Every politico is afraid one way or another.

That is how the one time successful businessman, President Donald John Trump, has for the last four years been left with a twitter handle for solace. Tweets are his defence. Tweets are the manner he vents out. Tweets are his consolation. And so when he is in panic, in the middle of the night *mostly* who wonders he tweets "COVFEFE"? Tweets are the way he reaches out and displays humility. His humour. An attempt to easy a boiling psyche. Poor Donald. An elected President battling the media since day zero in office. Some would break in circumstances less.

Those who have had no history lessons on or knowledge of power dynamics throughout civilizations miscomprehend and think the current president of the USA is a lackey. In truth he isn't. I would argue he is a clever fellow who was able to beat the Democrats in 2016 when he hadn't full backing of his party (the Republicans).

Left against a formidable opponent in the person of Hilary Rodham Clinton – she had the *actual* establishment – supported by the best rhetorician of our time, Barack Hussein Obama – then President of USA – Trump had *very* limited chances. Trump was a welterweight in a ring, facing Washington's heavy-weights. He had a divided public to contain. The Media, Pundits, Commentators, Cynics, Analysts and Academicians guffawed or hackled when on screens Trump made comments he would win the general elections. Some even dared shout he was out of his mind. Or that he was a disgrace to the US political class. An ama-teur they noted. He proved them wrong in his subtle ways. This we are witnesses of.

It was stunning when Donald Trump carried the day. Against establishment and brilliance of a sitting president's party. It was mind boggling. Some emotional citizens had sworn to leave the US if Donnie won. Wow! He won. And not popularly, using the circus, but technically it was. Through the path less travelled he fared. That was a taste of Trump's personal intel-ligence and mastery of plans execution. A master class of cal-culations, timing and knowledge of 'people and power'. Donald Trump and his cadres knew 'the people' own their emotions not the calculus of power as pollsters seemed to suggest.

Whatever the way you perceive the case, we know after win-ning, Donald Trump plummeted into popular disfavour. Tor-rent of insults were hurled upon his person. His biography was unearthed and bio-data made an issue. He became laughable to many *presumed* progressives and was denigrated in many ways possible. Cartoons sprang all over America equating him to a failure, a bigot, a misogynist, a bag of hot air and one full of himself. In riff raff outlets he was depicted a deadpan caressing female crotches. Online GIFs made his caricature busy sucking teen nipples. In others he appeared buying cheap prostitutes or attempting rape. He has been associated with complete lack of

America's virtues and neoliberal sophistication.

In all that the President was/still is enduring, the security agencies haven't stood by him or come to his aid – at least by allaying fabrications and sifting lies. They are not making *anything* easy for the man. It all seems, this far, that the agencies have had their conclusions drawn and path plotted. Therein is a dark secret. And that is why the president *somehow* thinks the spy agencies' credibility is doubtful. Pushed against the wall that much, who would not? It's hard. It is a wonder he hasn't been bulldozed this far.

Overlooking Has A Price

They say 'a journey of a million miles begins with a single step'. The assaults on the person of Donald Trump are but a start of a walk that will deal *many* blows to America's political traditions. It is palpable today as you read this that the 'acts' have graduated into big problems. For example, a number of staffers appointed to senior positions are rained with accusations of rape, bigotry, misogyny, hatefulness, racism, anti-Semitism, abuse of power or any other misconduct. Oblivious to millions of Americans is that deliberate laxity of security agencies is piling harms to their level of conscience. Targeted presidential appointees are slapped with criminal cases far-fetched. Whatever the spy agencies can recall/lay hands upon. Although an unsuspecting mass is being misinformed of the craft and thus misconstrue it, the purpose is to atone staunch 'elites' of some political streaks and mind-set.

Politicians are being shaped to fit what spy corps accredit or want for 'America'. This is the origin of *many* matrix projects – deliberate, engineered containing mechanics – that make sure spy agencies have top influencers of Americans follow *roughly* pre-destined paths.

That says: the spy agencies are running the public brain. They mainstream leading ideas and inhibit plurality and ranges of views. This concludes that none can freely project his views of society, politics and humanity strongly enough to re-train courses of people's imagination and initiatives. Imaginations and innovativeness are strictly scaled. The only place such inhibitions are let loose is in the academia – where of course ideas are born but quickly die silent deaths. So professors can write all they like and teach their theories to students – that is the furthest they get. Elsewhere, no. Unless ideas fit preconceived Intel matrix. Otherwise they are attacked.

The agencies are *in practice* bogging down the legacy of America's Age of Reason. And they don't see this is in itself an act of spelling doom.

Bogging down the popular conscience is one category of the many forms of blackmailing known. No question about that.

Leashing the people by use of one's socio-historical experience is the most successful subverting mechanics known this far. It is based on a *hominem* sort of argumentation i.e. attacking the person rather than appraising his argument's worth.

Given the nature a majority is raised and exposed to social dynamics (socialization processes), one must have something to be accused of. MUST is the word.

If a man's groping of a woman's crotch when they were indulgent teenagers or sophomores is enough of a scandal to bar someone from adult-age roles, well, no straight guy is eligible for a post. The US is so open and liberal a society none can predict *own* temporal behaviours. Psychologists (read Abbey Antonio, Friedman Richard and Sigmund Freud, for example) know well sexual misbehaviour (especially bullying, aggression) is a natural manifestation of the 'aggressiveness streaks' many virile young men are apt to – more so at some point(s).

Perhaps you will be surprised when I tell you, 'you are a rapist, good one'. Believe me, when the circumstances are right for it psychologists argue you will commit rape. It only needs a strong lead on. See for yourself as an example; the US alone, despite all knowledge of goodwill, humility and civility people have had has more than 1.3 million rapes a year. This is a glimpse of how complex the society is.

In America today *some* spy agencies dig people's past misdeeds 'to get to' whoever they want. Of course the agencies personify their being involved whilst lurking behind presumed victims. Unsuspecting common citizens then wonder why are such scandals many in years of elections or on occasion persons deemed 'controversial' assume or threaten power. The word 'controversial' is again *'weaponised'* to subdue some characters. In the beginning few socialites suffered the blackmail, then came artists and senior civil employees. That was the pilot phase. The actors grew relentless and kept improving it. Politicians shrugged it off – they thought it was none of their business. Now that the blackmail is fully perfected, every politician is in, afraid of his/her past. They now see they are the very fishes intended in the first place. To avoid the bait one such fat fish has to remain in deep waters – that is, lie low!

Whatever the 'conceivers' thought about this trick, well, history downgrades its underhanded manoeuvres as 'utter destructive' of civilizations. It is a medieval tactic and ways before that. Psychologists in modern time should be decrying it as a failure to comprehend many inconsistencies mankind is gifted. Man is essentially 'lawless and troublesome'. That is why civilizations make laws not to preserve some people's past to use for containment.

Internal Rifts And Their Allied Emergencies

From the foregoing one sees that there is something unwell about America's political societies. It is something hidden in the presumed divide between Democrats and Republicans. It would seem that the arrangement go beyond the two. America's partisanships and her vigorous party politics is a ruse that only myopic analysts do take serious. In reality, any democrat or republican who doesn't fall in favour of the military complexes' architecture is *potentially* a criminal. Someone can besmirch him down low.

The spy agencies can always dig something up against any

person. Thus the agencies have placed the US politician into a sort of political matrix. And, graciously, the judiciary will always step in to strike some judicial settlements for acquittal or waiver of indictment. See how clever the bargain is? That is the way they humble stubborn politicos or tone down anyone they choose. The target being either someone to calm down, to make one renege her previous standing, to influence one's course of decisions or to purvey particular roles in any character. With this setup America is losing the traditional, visionary and divergent thinkers who have been her politics' hallmarks. All this so they can get many orchestrated political deadpans.

Mostly, America is getting calculated populists raised from the dusts of intelligence files and quiet backroom profiling chambers.

In the next parts of these series you are going to read how this cunning was the route most empires took towards self-defeat. It is a hollow pipe. And it is not unique to the USA. Some tacticians out there in Washington consider that route useful or an edge they have but wow that is a course well exhausted in gone civilizations. It always has been a thin end of the wedge. There always comes a time powers start it out. A time politicians and military brasses think they are so clever that laws have to work for them. Yet laws are double-edged swords.

In reality politicians end up being the victims ... And then politics grow anarchic...

SECTION THREE: TELLTALES

*...in the Last Days of
America's Hegemony (6)*

A Cunning Military Complex Ever Seen

On a note that the military structure of the USA is past 'defence' rather 'offensive' very few can wonder. Again on the line of thought that the US military complex is becoming destructive than is constructive both internally and externally only the short-sighted can doubt.

Take the weaponry department's influence for example – you will prove any of those arguments.

The US military is 'fed' by a cunning weaponry department that is mainly – some can be surprised – non-governmental. Private money makers own the mills and stores of weapons. The US government thus buy from them. Say it again; the US Army gets its weapons from some privates. Call it the weapons' business. Or the gun mercantilism. It is an outsmarting arrangement of the highest calibre never before witnessed in the history of civilisations.

This is it: gun manufacturers that the US taxpayers (read: federal and state authorities) buy from are private enterprises. I insist: the Ministry of Defence's budget is all paid to private venturers holding shares or/and running manufacturing of war technologies – the likes of Lock Heed Martins, Boeing, Raytheon, Northrop Grumman, Heckler and Koch et al. They are numerous. This, in all honest, comes back to square one. That the US security system is an item for sale. By extension the whole world security is that way fated. Since the venturers must have their business rolling and turning in INCREASING profits, trouble is unavoidable. They must have in place a *vicious* scheme to do progressing gun businesses. For instance, terrorise the people and cheat them of their dimes. A scheme impossible without violence or any such threats. Schemes leading to appreciating sales of weapons.

To sell *widely* especially *globally* is the best part of the game. And this means global violence is the ace.

From some previous and later parts of this treatise I note that the gravity of the US imperialism lies in her military complex. I call the US supremacy 'a hegemony of military intelligence'. That is the highest notch she is. The first consumer of intellect the US academia, researchers and innovators of all wakes of life bring in is the military intelligence - that, faster than all others. The intelligence agencies are the enablers (lubricants) of her hegemony. The USA has a mighty Army spurred to actions by a double digit number of security, defence and spy agencies. The agencies are feeders of intelligence to the military, the Senate and Congress (say: all elites), the public and the judiciary. In the same vein I indicate that those agencies have conditioned both the political climate of America, the foreign policy environment and the ensuing public mind-sets. They do all those in ways far removed from the people's soggy conscience.

That is your FBI, CIA, NSA et al.

See, China may have so big a military body. Russia can amass millions of young fighters and India is so populous she can gather a staggering host. Well, that is true. The three can again equip their soldiers and train them days and nights, for years on end. Yet it is true they cannot, singularly, defeat the US as she is today. Why is that the case? It is because the extent of intelligence the US has put in her (military) efforts to control the rest of the world is insurmountable. The US beats her adversaries before she begins the physical wars. The Pentagon aces make wars in the mind of their enemies firsthand. When they send out the armies, the battles are almost won already. This comes from her superb use of military intelligences.

One learns, at least from the foregoing, that the intelligence agencies are the de facto disc jokers (DJs) that play the US imperial music. They pull clever feats and frame situations. They organise public thoughts through profiling personalities. They mudsling. They character-assassinate. They get their ways by tempering with the public opinions. All these mean that in most cases the agencies are the projectors of baseline views that guide politicians, lawyers and the public thought (*psyche*: ideation). Sum up: they rule. Here in, though, lies the danger of effective militarising. For in a clandestine way the US has the military complex ruling. Not public institutions.

Thus if it is in the army's interest the agencies create decoys and dully inform POTUS that Russia is giving chemical weapons to Syria. If the report is well-crafted and a cunning follow-up is made to foot the bill, the submission ought to inflame political divides and push for actions. Or, (some five years ago) they make an allegation that a tiny East African State – called Burundi – is carrying out a silent *genocide* on her people. All these were apt to lead to some strategic actions overseen and orchestrated by the military industry. The Army's intelligence had closely followed Russia's move to stand by the two states – Syria and Burundi. That was a cause for alarm. In any ensuing violent stance (as it happened in Syria) the weapon manufacturers smile all the way to the banks.

All those elucidated above are reminiscent of ancient Rome. In old Rome (whatever period one chooses) there were power for the abled army generals. They *virtually* possessed the legionnaires and the intelligence network. In practice they were the ones aware of peace and security climates. They had the mechanics and intelligence to interpret consequences of other polities' actions and thus would advise the Senate accordingly. They had and always applied some leverages. They were the ultimate power. When such generals were few, they could choose to cut deals – to syndicate power and grab the majority decisions. The first triumvirate between Gnaeus Pompey Magnus, Gaius Julius Caesar and Marcus Licinius Crassus was born out of such context. Decades later, other generals: Marcus Antonius (Mark Anthony), Gaius Octavianus (Augustus Octavian) and Marcus Aemilius Lepidus would emulate the pioneer triumvirs' act creating the second Triumvirate. The laurels of the Senate began and ended with debating some in-house blah blahs. Further than that the parroting Roman Senators worked for fat bribes to endorse premeditated military forays and some legal clauses conceived on behalf of the powerful Generals.

Many a time in Rome, the Consuls (begin from Scipio Africanus to Augustus Octavianus and his protégés) had to be top-notch Army generals. And they fared through an extensive endorsement system supported by a scheme/a social arrangement known as *Clientela*. An endorsement made possible through patronage. Well, the US patronage lies quietly within connections held in place by the lobbying machineries. And it is all Roman but in name.

Old Rome was in fact ruled by the Armies (the legions). And that became her eventual problem... For the powers of Armies hail from ceaseless military exploits. Rome grew 'warlike' all along. Rome would fight and fight and fight until she wore herself. America isn't doing any different...

Can Americans Decide Their Fate?

It depends on how far you are misled to believe. For America's illusion very much capitalises in *ideation* that what many know to be are not what they really are. In the immediate preceding issue I submit that the US president – or any other politician – is as well at the mercy of intelligence gatherers. Therein I beef up my arguments well enough. See this example, when the three preceding presidents lay the blame for presidential misdeeds, they name intelligence and military *files* having been the causes. Donald Trump has been showing this distrust *openly*. He often lambasts security agencies' claims as hoaxes and ill-intentioned. Barack Obama regretted (*openly*: he was being interviewed by the Atlantic News) of having been misled by intelligence on situations in Libya. Again, he says, 'it was okay to unseat Muammar Gaddafi but the end was poorly executed and thus the result wasn't what he had expected'. Obama single's out Libya as the worst mistake of his administration.

Well? Here Obama was either lying or he didn't know what he was talking about. Of course he knew the Libya manual had been used in Iraq against Saddam Hussein and before that in Afghanistan against the Taleban. Their files surely had graced Obama's table in the eight years he occupied the White House. He should have known. Same plans, same results. George W. Bush noted (*openly*) that he acted on false Intel about Iraq's (Saddam Hussein) chemical weapons. Bush identified that decision as "regrettable" admitting of having been misled.

Now the POTUS is the first citizen of USA. If (as we see in the cases above) he can be mixed up then who is spared? Surely not the simpletons/citizens. They are left grappling with the woes of the acrobatics/tourneys between incomes and expenditures. This as the military walks away for field excursions. And the Arms manufacturers swing their credit cards in the air in pomp, celebrating new arrivals to their JPMorgan Chase accounts.

Amongst the commoners – average to low income citizens I mean – none is powerful to demand guns off streets either. Guns' circulation is taken for granted although no citizen can satisfactorily argue why. Of late, killings that are in all reasonableness terrorism, madness and senselessness are fraying. Children are being shot at '*en masse*' in schools and at social functions. One time they followed back-to-back it was horrible, terrifying. To insult the president, that month's killings frayed (that was the deadliest September, it was in 2015) in his Chicago South Side. The POTUS could literary hear (as per his own words) the wails of mothers and grandmothers. The president, Barack Obama, could not take it any more. The world saw their *lovely* Obama crying in public – his tears showing and telling the White House's inadequacy to quell the 'gunners' appetite for dollars.

Until today (five years after Obama presidency) tens are being killed in public by loitering gun owners. There is a lot of assaults done in public and are majority tagged to ownership of guns. Who in USA is courageous enough as to take guns off streets? No one. Obama could only break *openly* and blame Congress – which was all he ever did. This is because gun sales earn fat cheques for the US weaponry investors – and the weaponry *'money-baggers'* are better 'citizens' than the President and Congress combined. In reality the US gun manufacturers are trading lives. But most intelligence analyses have it that the problem isn't gun ownership. Wow! America's logic is way too bright, I wish I were an ignorant student.

You want a horrifying peep, perhaps? Well, make follow-ups on how Intelligence agencies, Congressional and Senatorial committees discuss the problem of gun killings. You will swear America's elites are born pretenders, worshippers of money. Money making is their goddess. As you listen to their arguments life suddenly seems cheap and inconsequential. Whereas the bucks loom large as the thing to live and die for.

That guns are no cause for street killings they argue. The President, the Senators and the Congress are vehemently in support of continued gun selling no matter how many commoners are losing lives. To woo the market even more, guns are becoming cheaper and more widespread. One must respect the US when it comes to money making. The Houses' early seating to discuss any serious submission start with clashes over the issue's pecuniary implication. That cleared, only that time, does anything else follow. Another evidence America is off tracks... as long as money shines...

...in the Last Days of America's Hegemony (7)

The Money And Politics Of This Superpower

I wrote 'Money and Politics have made humans the "indignant desert birds". My reference for the words 'indignant desert birds' was from W.B. Yeats' poem 'The Second Coming'.

I personally take it that where the world is today 'we are the indignant birds Yeats wrote about back in 1919'. We live in a desert (albeit virtual one) caused by our being slaves of money...of power... of politics. And this we are surely going to pass on to the next generations. In this respect, America leads the pack – after all she is the superpower, the coach. The knower of all things. I say the jack of all trades.

Big economy notwithstanding, Americans are deeply indignant – and somehow getting totally frustrated. The US is no longer herself. Sadly many foreigners cannot see this so they are migrating en masse to America. Well, 'grass is greener on the other side, till you get there and see it for yourself'... so sings Lucky Dube in his vibrant, cool release "The Other Side".

Everywhere thousands of 'the wretched of the earth' are trekking off leaving their homes miles onshore. Some are leaving because their desert shrub lands have been made worse by America's bombing or any other of her great *Sherlock-Holmesing*. Crossing very choppy seas they are doing. Braving the Seas that either kill, harass or desecrate them. It depends on what marine devil is on duty that day. Desecration is rampant though. What, for example, is worse than being parent(s) to an emigrant boy washing dead to the beach? The poor kid. Poor Alan Kurdi! An innocent kid *tangled* amongst blasting bombers: the *Bs* and the *Tupolevs* and threatened by monstrous *Altays*. The poor boy is a tale of how nefarious the global economy is riding. And a tell-tale that economic 'powers' are overburdening the generations. Before money ruled the earth children used to die in honour.

America's money (the dollar bills, the 'smackers'), the military powers and the politics have become the most sadistic ever. History bears witness to her incomparable manoeuvres. For the first time in human history the world has seen a hegemony wherein the enduring factors of might: the military capability, the intelligence, sharp reason, manipulative economics, guileful academia, excessive knowledge, superb science and technology and skilful humanism have come together to speak one tongue. They are speaking the language of 'money' – the dollar bills owned by the Federal Reserve System are singing. Money is power. Power is politics. Therefore, Money is politics. Philosophers would thus apply the Euclidian axiom: "things which are equal to the same thing are equal to each other". No recorded empire before the USA has had similar kind of the mergers amongst those enduring factors.

Be honest, say for instance, why are the sanctimonious US Senate, Congress and Judiciary not banning guns from civilian neighbourhoods? Instead, see, there doubles technical improvement of weapons (and their mass production) to lower the unit prices and/or attract new orders. Interpret this in practice of the evident gun uses going on in the US: the more the killings the more is growing the appetite for selling better guns – so to say.

The most offered justification for US gun business (sales to the public) is that with the weapon people can do self-defence timely and remain in control of their security. Yet recently very few, if any, have reportedly died defending themselves using their guns. The killers happen to be some predominantly adept 'Jack the Rippers' who kill before the victims know it. The possibility a citizen can defend himself because he/she has a gun is extremely minimal and would depend on chance mostly. Trained fighters, especially battle hardened soldiers, well know one of the most important elements of successful attack is 'surprise'. With surprise, a weak adversary can outsmart and even subdue a superior, well trained opponent. This is because the act of attacking happens so fast the first distraction any victim has is *likely* his last.

In most attacks, the early shooters are at advantage. This because before they make the slightest move they must have had clear conscience of their deeds. They happen to have planned and put in place best logistics to help execute their targets. This include earmarking the crime scene in advance and closely studying patterns, changes and movements related to their ultimate intention. The more skilled a killer is the better and more detailed preparation he makes. After being sure of all that there is to know, they choose their weapons, necessary supplies, arrange (or rehearse) timing and then designate positions they will hold to achieve maximum results. If anything out of crucial contingencies happens, the killer can cross his fingers and take his time. All these, combined with the advantage of surprise, help killers to achieve their end. Which in most cases is killing as many victims as possible.

All the aforesaid are to the disadvantage of a gun owner who falls an abrupt victim, without having had the slightest hint he/she would be caught in an awkward situation. To many people in social places e.g. synagogues, schools and taverns fate strike from blue skies i.e. without a clue. A killer walks in and the moment any one guesses what is going on the gun is blazing past half magazine.

If the Congress and the Senate do ever (which I doubt they do) assume gun ownership can help people do self-defence that is the weirdest thought they ever had. It is disproven by almost all existing references – even those whose victims involved trained, combat-inured soldiers. The mass shooting at Fort Hood on November Five 2009 is exemplary. It proves amongst others that the best defence of the victim(s) goes way beyond possession of guns – for the Fort Hood incidence took place in the military premise (full of guns). And those killed were seasoned soldiers *some* were there ready for deployment or had just left operations.

At the Texas based Army Post, the 14 soldiers killed and the 30 wounded had high courage and (many had) superior training compared to the killer – US Army Major and Psychiatrist Nidal Hassan. The assassin had edges though: one, he had surprise on his side. Two, he had had enough time to plan everything before he moved. His victims had nothing to compensate – and those were big differences.

Probe it a note higher: why are killing sprees rising in USA despite her growing sophistication in Intel mechanics and related assemblages?' A fact about the US Intel is that security 'tracking payload' and Intel 'operation precision and speed' are astoundingly 'hi-tech'. The US spy agencies have at their disposal a spectrum of mechanics, expertise, software, tracing assemblages, operation models and techniques nudging perfection. Yet bloodbaths (in the streets, social spaces and public halls) are becoming frequent. They are *now* eying regularity. Ask why. The answer doesn't come straight. Critical analysts argue that details of intelligence and technology are weighed between 'money and power'. Not safety and/or harmony. They are of the opinion that this is the root of America's security problem as we see it now. Money making is the bloom.

Look, guns make money. Not security. The US political establishment is a hostage to the weaponry manufacturers. Politicians earn big time from that business – it is contended. That they oversee a form of gun mercantilism. That is it.

Naturally a gun is used 'to gun' and 'gunning' means 'taking down lives'. Killing it is! This is violence. Absent violence guns do not (and cannot) work. Contenders in this school of thought thus have a thread that suggests the problem of gun violence in USA, now being shipped abroad, is hinged upon gun profiteering. They show that with billions of money involved in the gun business triangle no Senator or Congressman can take guns off streets...

And if no one can take guns off American streets, the neighbourhoods in which US toddlers play their childhood, one is crazy to ever think the same US politicians can envision 'peaceful hamlets' where the Alan Kurdis come from. For charity begins home, *ma'am*. 'A man who lets fire raze his homestead cannot lend hand to his neighbour in the same' – says my people's adage. America's cruelty seen abroad is thus a manifestation of her disintegrating internal safety. A form of moral irresponsibility that involves trade in violence.

The Liability The Us Intelligence Is

Whether internally or externally operating the US Intelligence agencies must use 'the people' for field training. They work amongst, for, with and by the people. Public anomalies are their boons. There they gather information, cook, simulate scenarios and orient the people towards directions they are focusing on (*read* Julian Assange). Or more candidly listen Mike Pompeo: "I was the CIA director. We lied, We cheated, We stole". It is this way they earn immediate and prolonged trusts on *issues* and expand departmental budgets and/or influence decision makers. Outsmarting them. Lying to them. This way they invented the current misinformation that is now a global concern.

An incidence like the 9/11 was to the agencies a blessing in disguise. It warranted *issuance* of hard federal money and expanded expenditure on the military and spy operations. It gave spy hierarchies and the military 'kingpins' powers to arm-twist whoever they wanted. It also gave them power to invade any territory they picked anywhere, anyway, anyhow. A giant leeway, see? The label applicable now is simple, 'she is a threat to national security' or they designate a group, a country or an organization 'terrorist'. Or 'an axis of evil'.

The September Eleven incidence is one event that would be studied longer if the world were not in this mess of disinformation we have today. It is an incidence that has had no equal in the recent annals of events. Sadly, there was disinformation before there came that incidence – and there was denial before all. Thus even when one has solid evidences to argue there were many people who knew and perhaps planned the incidence, one ends up being a 'conspiratorial' author and all that. So the historical importance of the event of 9/11 has dimmed over time and is less scholarly analysed this far.

It is twenty years since the blowing and wiping out of lives occurred and there is little (mainly fame of barbarism) those responsible (as alleged, Al-Qaeda et al) have gained but systematic deaths of their ranks. This whilst the victim (the USA) has immensely benefited and will benefit for a long time. The US allies – Europe largely – have been smiling all the way to the banks (since 2001). To cut a long story short, no serious scholar should lightly take the 9/11 incidence. For no one can explain the world as it is today without referring to the event's aftermath. More so if it is an economic or security analysis.

There is this gem lying in the dusts of many books – it is called the principle of parsimony. Many scholars call it the Occam's razor – named after one English Franciscan friar, William of Ockham. It is a tool of getting knowledge (problem-solving) through the use of very simplified routes, explanation and thought. As an insult on the behaviour of complex things, Occam's razor tells that 'all complex things have very simple solutions'. That is, if you want to know anything that is seemingly complex, inquire its simplest thoughts possible. It will breakdown and melt into thin veils you can see through.

I tend to use that principle when I think the gloomy September Eleven. An incidence that involved few terrorist (only 19) suicides hijacking few planes (four planes actually) to ram them into iconic US buildings – the WTC and the Pentagon. In the incidence, less than three thousands died and more were crippled. Then there were thousands of orphans created out there in the streets and razing down of less than five blocks of buildings that are nowhere close to twelve billion US dollars. The disruption to the US economy was not felt – neither did the air flights stop nor the US production sector grind to a halt. So, the supposed terror act only succeeded to induce temporal fear and some ruptures here and there. In sum, all it achieved was a little 'sadism'.

What followed that sadness on the side of the US and her allies were quite different.

The US called upon all her allies and the world telling each of them to stand 'either on her side or her enemy's'. In a blink of an eye, the US was commanding the world and the allies were all there at her side flexing their muscles.

From there onwards money mines opened and they would remain ajar for decades....

First, the world was slapped with an urgent need to restructure security instruments, rules and guidelines. ASAP the global nations did and that involved some overhauls in domestic rules, security and traditions. Yet this was an undertaking that only the US and her allies would review and say 'yeah, you did well' – not a country's own security audit. And a majority of the changes further the US interference in a host of other nations' internal security functioning, capacity and expertise. For example, any perceived security threat with a hint of terrorism must immediately be informed to Interpol and the latter whisper that to CIA and FBI. So what do we have today? We have a system wherein the CIA can at any moment know what secret is going on in another country if it wants – a false flag is all it takes. And there are other subtle traps in place.

Second, in the wake of 9/11, see, the world was hammered with '*trillionaire*' investments – this is the quickest money ever made in world history. What was that? It was the money the world was forced to part with in a couple of years to procure and beef up security gears and technologies. This is it: airports all over the world were to be refitted, resupplied with new security instruments, gadgets and communication sets. Surveillance technologies are very expensive but each nation was immediately expected to procure them – no compromise. Planes were sent back to hangars in the West mainly to be renovated, reconfigured and remodelled to ensure security – for instance, altering direct physical communication between passengers and pilots. This to ensure no passenger can again ever commandeer a plane and force the pilots to change course. If you travel through any international airport today, the threatening security procedures you go through are majority results of post 9/11. And they cost millions of USD to acquire, fit, run and maintain.

Third, go back to 2001 and think. The September Eleven incidence occurred at a time almost 85% of the technologies that airports, planes, surveillance and public installations' security needed were technologies only the USA and few nations in Europe had. So the recipients of each coin from all that was needed was either in US, Canada or Europe. Countries like Japan hadn't made much strides in that area. Chinese corporations that had franchises in that business either were very few or had their technological licenses in the West. Little can be said of Russia and India.

One can now see that in a span of twenty years, the ensuing technological needs/scrambles almost globally sent trillions of $ to either America or Europe. This is a revenue that surpasses what any other investment could generate in a period of a hundred years. But the 9/11 netted the money in less than two decades.

Last, the 9/11 brought in the current security blanket that only the West – under the US leadership – can use. For example, the US can single out a national agency of another country – say the Iranian Revolutionary Guards Corps – and call it a terrorist group. And subsequent to that the US can move to kill an IRGC's commander (Gen. Qasem Soleimani, then named a terrorist mastermind) without hiding any part of the plot. No other country can ever do that without becoming a demonised state. So now, how do you view the September Eleven?

Me: if the Al – Qaeda ever planned and executed that act – which I am not saying it wasn't capable of – Qaeda's economic advisers and strategists should this far be scratching their heads in shame. There has never been a flop, a bad planning I mean, wherein the planner gives the best opportunity to his enemy the way the terror group did in 2001. They actually acted against themselves. To this day, Saud Arabia is in a precarious position she might one day suffer some forms of legal retribution – some strokes, given that her citizens allegedly masterminded and executed the incidence. You see now why Arabia is all this time dotting on the 'Stateside'. The event gave an upper hand and an economic haven to Qaeda's enemy. It gave USA money and power...

'Money and Power' are the ultimate destinations in the US political contours – not Qaeda's, we know well.

The US military nexuses use their huge budgets and robust technological muscles to frisk any nation and group they want. Any such episode earn extra money for the weaponry department. Tens intelligence agencies are busy freaking global political climate, people's imagination and profiling contextual events to engineer the populace towards courses which give way to militarisation.

It wouldn't in any way surprise any one that the 9/11 was such a flip and a profiling master class. Following that incidence even the US *police* departments would later be *militarised*. That is, armed more or less like military units. It is simply a matter of time before the US makes sure all police contingencies on earth are militarised – because she has to make sure her gun mercantilism is well keyed in.

Public imaging is invested deep, if not deeper, in American society. Even the film industry is engineered towards such hegemonic path. It's building an epic public image through 'audio-visuals'. It caters to the image the public should give its sons and daughters. Many movies your kids watch are feeders of projected militaristic milieu. One shouldn't overlook this. Do this quiz: talk to your kid the moment she finishes watching a Star Wars season, a Ben Ten: The Aliens or any such movie and hear what she has to say. The baby will offer you a very grandiloquent view of gigantic, heroic proportion to a direction of a conqueror. The movies earn money yet they paste grand images and imaginations (the exact reasons the US heavily funds the industry). It is a purveyor of future heroes. The directors and producers are responsible with manufacturing soldiers who will later go to die in foreign lands playing 'Captain America', 'Superman', 'Spiderman', 'Commando', 'Rambo' etc. That is power. Tempering with the young minds as they grow. It is the truest source of power the USA masters better.

Through playing the jack of all trades, the US military complex has the people in indignations and incomprehensible despairs. Dreams scratch frustrations. The fear of unknown violence, for example, encourage gun sale for self-defence. Yet guns pour in more frustrations as behaviours of the people become unpredictable. It is complicated *than* it sounds. The complications explain why Americans – and global victims of US militarisation – are droves of indignant birds. The power of intellect *now* applied by the US agencies is way past common sense. It gets PhDs nicely gullible and grappling with the obvious. It leaves the earth worried at best. You need to be much of an ignorant not to feel it. The US imperialism has created a controversially rumbling civilisation. A civilisation based on idealism… a mistake…

A Fact: Civilizations Were Here Before The Usa

Although polities – and subsequently nations, empires, civilizations and dominions – are first built from people's efforts, immense preoccupation with money/wealth making or/and construction of solid powers have been the routes to self-defeat. This is a glaring fact in histories of imperial powers. Again, civilizations do not crumble from without until they have started faltering from within. Why is this eternally a fact? Because money and power give leeway to the cunning money-driven-crazies (call them money *addicts*). These are the 'goblins' manufactured by the society as it transforms through the levels of polity, nation, empire, civilisation and dominions (colonies). This is the first tell-tale. It seemingly is subtle yet of a very serious note.

Next, the money addicts are naturally ambivalent, that is,

they don't settle with issues but blow off into the spirit of endless-money-making leagues. But money needs power and more power brings more money. The two are complimentary. Hence the ambivalence feature. And this circumstance traps a civilisation. Such spirit makes the money addicts a malignant lot – malevolent. Malevolent human souls (as a rule of nature) are selfish. They end up needing the whole world for themselves. As per historical precedents, this takes some forms of global monopolisation. But soon or later the lot of malignant money-addicts recognise that 'the sea of humanity' is so complex and perilously energetic it is unconquerable. Partly conquerable yes but not into total submission. Ancient civilizations wherein lived people like Cyrus and Darius of Persia, Phillip II and his son Alexander III of Macedonia, Lucius Sulla and his rival Gaius Marius of Rome, Gaius Caesar and his adopted son, *divi filius*, Augustus Octavian etc. all bear witnesses to this unconquerable human nature. I expound on this nature in the last four parts.

The import of later articles in this treatise is to show that the US hegemony is not following a unique path. The parts pinpoint how other powers have had their rolls *in almost the same way* before they were gone. Through comparing previous instances with the Washington today we learn that the US is already downwind of imperial missteps. She is in her last days. The days hold steadfastly on 'confusing one's own people', 'throwing them off tracks of *renowned* civilities ... becoming the jack of all trades... etc. Empires end up building very confusing edifices as the means to steal other nations' treasures. They end up confusing themselves as well...

They become that "... hopeless sinner(s) who has hurt all mankind just to serve his own (belief)"... so sings Bob Marley in his outstanding "One Love".

The Falcon Cannot Hear The Falconer

The US is already downwind of imperial decline. This can smoothly be argued with reasonable evidences, lessons from what went on in history and temporal (periodically fettered, I mean) comparisons that leave no want.

For instance, the last days of each imperial guard now gone necessarily involved: investing in confusing her people and throwing them off tracks... becoming the jack of all trades... And each imperial power regarded herself owner of the best ideas, best economy and best philosophies of power. Each empire again determined that others had to follow her social philosophies. And hence vied to ascertain that. This last is hubris. And the rest were the reasons powers at last desired and pushed for respect from others instead of negotiating them as equals. Isn't America here yet?

I don't need your answer...

There are varying, debatable perspectives on evidences for the impending decline of the mighty USA as a global head prefect – there are domestic and globalist perspectives. Yet most scholars would agree the serious challenges her hegemony face today are internal. That the political elites are no longer catering to their benefactor. For example, politicos are investing in confusing their own people (the basic agenda herein being to manipulate them) on fundamental issues. This approach to politicking has left the people torn in despair, confusion, resentment, distrust and helplessness. Take disinformation strategy as an example: millions of innocent citizens are fed wrong information daily and they cannot know otherwise. The matrix that misinforms the public is a complex mix that was well knit before the people had a clue. A lot of authors before me have been warning about this as much as they can.

Disinformation is being used by the politicians, the PR institutions, the spy agencies and of course the media corps. The news is now *chiefly* peddling lies. This is leading to some circumstances likely to kill America (a society erstwhile built on affirmed knowledge). The worse thing is Americans are getting false informed by the very professionals they traditionally depended up on e.g. distinguished experts, researchers, scientists, professors, medical doctors etc. The lobbying corp. is using all the brains possible to mislead the multitude.

The Lobbyists are enriching professors, scientists and all good people through a machinery trading lies and a lot of hypotheses yet to be proven. Let us call it a *'stupidifying'* conduit.

As of politicians' lies and cabal mechanics of political *wizardry*, the truth has over the Ages remained the same: 'if the people cannot connect to the philosophies of power espoused by their state (politicians), a civilization unavoidably crumbles'. A read on this is abundant in history books.

Confusing the people as per their nation's place, manifests and political thought first and foremost erode the spirit of patriotism. Yet patriotism (an *illusion* with great impact throughout history) is the foundation of personal sacrifice. No man would ever tear away his *precious* life for another people (fellow citizens) if not for that illusion.

All throughout the history of mankind it would seem that for a polity to hold the reins of power successfully her people must, first of all, have had clear conscience of who they were and where they were headed. As a result the decision politicians undertook (in the name of nationhood) translated into *final* decisions for fate and destiny. Destiny of the people. That outlook bred patriotism.

Patriotism as a word comes for the Greek *'pater'* which means 'father'. Romans would alter the word to Latin *'patres'* which again means father. But since the early days that word somehow associated a father to a native land. Patriotism thus came to mean 'love of the native land'. A mother was another case; she was not necessarily bound to the native land - she could marry and move away. A princess could for example go to marry a distant prince and rightly become the queen of that land far off.

With the reality of 'nativity' in mind people lived and died under the banners of their nations – just as a lovely son would willingly sacrifice fighting for the life and love of a father. See, America is no longer towing this line of illusion. Recent researches, for example, show that Donald Trump won his 2016 election partly because the people in states a majority of soldiers *then in wars* come from overwhelmingly voted Trump (not to confuse the man with the Republican Party).

Researchers found out that voters had considered Trump rogue enough he could break away from Washington's aggressive tradition – thus, one to tear them from the vicious cycle of wars that are making their sons crippled under a false belief in patriotism. Here now the State has troubles from the falconer. For such feeling is a farewell bid to a hegemon. Growing against warring is contrary to what happens in the lives and times of hegemons, especially ones of military intelligence... One like the USA.

Sheer Uncertainty

From the simplest decision that guns should be off streets because they are dangerous to 'life' and the acknowledgement that 'men are not women' Americans are gagged as to what is what. Cabals hiding behind administrative curtains maintain gun sale business because it generates private wealth and the popular conscience cannot force otherwise. The population is leashed, that is all.

The decision is egoistic for one. It is economic for two. Egoistic because America's political classes: Congress, Senate, Governors or any other top administrator is rarely exposed to acts of loitering gun violence. It thus remains a problem for commoners roaming the streets. The political class is thus inclined to see it in a third party-view and hence of less concern to them. On the second note, a US politician is lobbied with cash or influence to adopt legislations. The gun industry has hard cash. The taxman collects beefy revenues from gun sellers and the industries. So a gun is money. Hard cash. The politicians receive sound federal receipts to present to the public to silence them.

It is economy.

The same politicians preach 'homosexuality is healthy'. People are stunned. Because they have all over the generations known that sodomy is an abomination that destroyed civilisations over the Ages. And the US politicians, faced with the task to justify *scientifically* how healthy can be 'rectal sperms' that homosexuality necessarily yields to, the politicians rely on some *socially constructed* explanations we read in the LGBTQ publications.

Yet they know scientifically speaking; no one can validate homosexuality using concrete, empirical and verifiable data. It has been tried but was a failure. That is why when Uganda gathered her brilliant scientists and consulted others from different parts of the world to advise on homosexuality, the scholar-doctors, overwhelmingly insisted it had no sound scientific base. They found no gene combinations, chemical processes or reactions that trigger homosexuality. President Museveni publically presented the doctors' advice and asked if there were any other who knew better to put forward evidences to the contrary. No one anywhere on earth was able to. Neither the Ugandan foolhardy activists who think they know much nor the global advocates submitted anything.

In the US, politicians were closely following that development in Kampala and they frothed anger warning Uganda this or that. Museveni had made a brilliant feint. One of pretending to move on to sign the anti-gay law before he suddenly stalled announcing he would wait for more scientific evidences before signing the bill. But the US and European donors had read the move – saw that he was dragging them to an argument they couldn't win. They avoided arguing their scientific facts – choosing to avoid the essence of the fracas. They knew it would bring tremendous reviews, critiques and dissatisfaction (with the results) globally. So they coiled from Museveni's provocation. But Uganda wanted to prove a point to the world and that deserved kudos.

Uganda then declared that she was banning and outlawing any gay practices following scientific evidences it was a social (self-construction by individuals) construction. As one would expect, the US and the West generally swiftly came over Uganda guns full blazing – no aids, no loans they threatened. Their remaining piece of logic and sense of reason – denying aids to the poor! They were ready to destroy the economy and the life of the people of Uganda for disagreeing on homosexuality. Just for taking a stand as is rightful of a sovereign.

But Museveni, of all his weaknesses, had proven his point. That it is a mere tactical kind of manoeuvre the West has come up with – not any genetic, hereditary or biological discovery whatsoever. He eventually put it in the following words,

> *"There's now an attempt at social imperialism, to impose social values. We're sorry to see that you (the West) live the way you live but we keep quiet about it".*

Yeah, Bob Marley's "… *hopeless sinner(s) who has hurt all mankind just to serve his own (belief)*".

Actually, homosexuality is contrary to the systematic, very gradual and unmistakable centrifugal character of evolutionary paths. Sincere evolutionary scientists will agree. Evolution amongst species is for improved *chance of survival* – homosexuality doesn't seem to be that. It doesn't entail the slightest chance of improved proactivity or survival, no. The so called 'homosexuality is healthy' revolves around a need to achieve 'equality' and "happiness". Civil, legal equality and happiness that the US constitution and paragraph two of the declaration of independence posits. It was born out of the need to please the US's revered texts. The famous paragraph reads (in part):

> *"We hold these truths to be self-evident, that all men are created equal, that they are endowed by their Creator with certain unalienable Rights that among these are Life, Liberty and the pursuit of Happiness..."*

That is. Yet any blind or excessive pursuit of happiness – hedonism it is called – is well known to end up in trouble. This is a truth unquestionable from time immemorial. It is found in great works like Aristotle's 'golden mean' and 'epicureanism' by Epicurus. Since around 305 BC Epicurus of Athens and his followers (Hedonists) warned that the pursuit of pleasures – happiness – was a thing to be restricted. They observed that *most* pleasures are dynamic. That is to say, pleasures lead to something else and hence end up being destructive. The leading amongst destructive pleasures, Epicureanists continue, are physical satisfactions. Sex is named in there and is well discussed.

Exempting the easy majority who has no time to bother following up development of such issues – the now trending US political guile – any responsible critic can learn this and subsequently see it for what it is. 'Homosexuality is a human right' was born out of the inadequacy of a Texas State law when the landmark case, 'Lawrence v. Texas, 539 U.S. 558 (2003)' found that a lower Court judgement against partners found doing adult consensual intimacy (oral and/or anal – in privacy) violated liberty under the due Process Clause of the Fourteenth Amendment. The questions for appeal were presented at the Supreme Court as follows:

> *"Do the criminal convictions of John Lawrence and Tyron Garner under the Texas "Homosexual Conduct" law, which criminalizes sexual intimacy by same-sex couples, but not identical behaviour by different-sex couples, vio-*

*late the Fourteenth Amendment guarantee of equal pro-
tection of laws? Do their criminal convictions for adult
consensual sexual intimacy in the home violate their
vital interests in liberty and privacy protected by the Due
Process Clause of the Fourteenth Amendment? Should
Bowers v. Hardwick, 478 U.S. 186 (1986), be overruled?"*

The defence attorneys for Lawrence, as the case questions above read, had moved from defending their clients based on 'acts contravening the Texas law' to attack the Texas law now considered being in violation of the Fourteenth Amendment. Yes, it was in the Appellate jurisdiction (Supreme Court) and the contention was on point of law. If they attacked and successful proved the law wanting, it would be easy to invalidate the judgement that had found Lawrence and Garner (rightful) guilty. There were other important observations made by the Supreme Court (in that case) all to the effect that the Texas law: one, violated the Fourteenth Amendment guarantee of equal protection of laws. Two, that criminal conviction for adult consensual sexual intimacy in the home violate vital interests in liberty and privacy protected by the Due Process Clause of the Fourteenth Amendment. An additional observation is that the Texas law singled out same sex acts leaving out similar acts between consenting adults of different sexes (male and female). Which was a rightful observation that the same acts (anal and oral intimacy) pass between men and women in privacy, but the law is silent. The defendants here netted the law.

That way Lawrence and Garner were cleared of wrong doing and that was the beginning of it all. If you can, review that case closely you will learn where the US legal homosexuality (now a global wave named 'human right') came from and it wasn't anything to do with science. It isn't legality issue either – it ensued from the perceived 'unconstitutionality' of the Texas law when weighed against provisions of the Fourteenth Amendment of the US constitution: Due Processes and the Right to Privacy.

The quorum had nine judges who voted 6-3 in favour of defence but even in that instance dissenting judges decried the interpretation offered by majority opinion Anthony M. Kennedy. To many the interpretation was decried as a conspiracy of a sort rather than being a rational inquiry into conflict of laws. There was an *allegation* by some commentators that the 'senior most judge' on the bench had deliberately chosen 'majority opinion' under suspicious circumstance - that of knowing what Kennedy's stance was on the matter. And so *perhaps* Kennedy opined towards his alter ego.

Then there came this pretence and arrogance that the US constitution cannot be faulted (or the Texas law proved right instead) now causing 'third world' activists to dump their moral heads and traditions to be on the wagon. Hundreds of thousands of intellectuals globally *now* call it a *human* right, but little do they say how it ever came to be *humanly, right* or *genetically*. The gullible lot as usual. Instead of reworking (making clear) the US Constitution or relevant laws following the Supreme Court's *ratio decidendi* in Lawrence v. Texas, the White House rounded up the world and nations were pushed to change their laws and constitutions instead – saying 'homosexuality equal rights', 'homosexuality human rights'.

Sheer arrogance, that is. The US is raping the world!

There is no scientific base for homosexuality, this far. The world has seen it come and go all over the Ages – from the ancient societies to the present. And one factor about it has remained constant: it plays out more evident in societies when they grow too obsessed with hedonism – as a result of excessive material wealth.

All throughout history, the rise and fall of public sodomy is strictly attributed to mature, easy and developed societies with disparities so high. Whether one inquired Babylonia, Persia, Macedonia and Rome they all experienced high, open homosexuality when their societies were at the height of powers, freedoms and wealth. It has remained that way to date.

And almost uniformly, past civilisations either overlooked

it, played it low or called it an abomination. Before the USA today it is in old Sodom and Gomorrah alone where we are informed by the Bible that homosexuality had been publicised and legalised. At least here historians can be brave enough to say yes. And they can say the USA is speeding into *open* homosexuality from the time she achieved her imperial height in 1980s. Way before that sodomy remained illegal and strictly muted – mostly viewed as a kind of nuisance on the society. One they could push out of mind and relax. They had been shrugging it off countless times. So it remained one of the many social inconsistencies they could overlook and decry.

From 1980s that approach became no longer tenable as the mature capitalist society heartily moved from self-mortification. It is sinking deep in personal pleasures and the viles of individualism… Here we are.

I don't want to mean, at any point in this book, that homosexuality should have remained outlawed. That would contradict my understanding of society – especially the last days of mature empires. I know most empires' waning featured gross moral decay and social irresponsibility. Be it so in USA. Why would she be exceptional? Gosh! Yet I don't want to mean it should have been legalised. Because that would again contradict my conscience on what really makes a strong, enduring polity. Moral responsibility and affirmation amongst others are the ones that make a nation strong. I am stuck there.

Not even the judges sitting on the bench in Lawrence v. Texas said homosexuality should be legal, no – actually some of them went on to decry the decision and called it "continuing moral decay of the US society". I am a realist on this – I am submitting these facts in their black and whiteness.

All I want to insist here is, it should be called what it is – a social manifestation (some lawyers in USA use the words 'social decay') arriving in our Age. Just like it manifested in Ages gone.

Sodomy is cyclic: it hibernates and it springs to life times on times off. It is part of a continuum. And it is a people's construction. Not genetic. It is constructed presently – a baffling attempt to most – for the need to ensure people's 'equality' as stated in the US declaration of independence.

It is baffling to allege that scientific realities guarantee the laws. It is baffling that after Texas laws got faulted, some scientists are brave enough to talk the world into homosexuality science blah blahs. How insane that is! It would be the first time in human history wherein failure of laws ever got used to discover an underlying biological nature. So far that nature is not yet known.

Well, there is no instance in nature *itself* wherein 'evolutionary paths' bother with equality. Equality in biological compositions? No. Not at all. We know equality isn't a factor for existence either. Our friends in a school called 'existentialism' would tell it better. They say; 'we live and take advantage of each other because we differ'. Life would be impossible without variations. Differences (variations/absence of equality) and defects seem to be the law of averages. Defects (mainly through *mutations*) seem to be the truest compositions nature has in store.

Human being is better placed because she can rationalise on the meaning of variations and choose the best possible. This is what 'survival of the fittest' represents. That there exists those who fit particular set of realities – those will survive. They will propagate their existence. That there exists those who fall short – thus ones who cannot further propagate their existence. There seems to exist a whole spectrum.

Nature is merciless. Very merciless. An example: nature has made you a fertile woman but left millions out there who won't see their offspring. A man: while you can enjoy a bed with your woman, there are millions out there who can never taste it all through their lives because they haven't had that gift of nature. Sadistic nature, uh! I feel for them yet I cannot advise that the best solution would be to push nature, for example, practice homosexuality to get a fuck. After all if the ancients were anything sensible they advised that 'very few problems really mean the end of life'. I believe missing an ability to have sex the straightway isn't one of them. Yet that is my humble view. You are entitled to yours without any qualm.

Me: when you seek biological equality you get to war with nature.

Skewed Realities

When the US Congress agrees for a war or interference with other nations' matters the people are at war... This is whether the people have feelings for or against such war(s). In several instances, the US citizens demonstrated, rallied or buzzed against some wars. The war in Iraq, Vietnam and Korea are few examples. Representatives in the Congress are in practice not representing... They almost always tend to part ways with the people. Thus eroding further the people's pride in a working democracy. Or having them uncertain of what the Congress do.

If you read recollections from war veterans or families of the fallen you realize up to date many aren't sure why there was the war(s) they fought in. Many decry of having been taken unaware and that *by then* they couldn't even explain why/how the poor people they found themselves fighting had become enemies. Go on arguing them and you will find this fall-back, 'we were defending the stars-and-stripes' – a pointing referring to the US flag. Indulge this a bit: defending the stars-and-stripes? Soon explanations become murky and meaningless. For they don't really know.

Well note that to date the US has around 28,500 troops stationed in the Korean Peninsula waiting for a war. Defending the stripes, again? The force is there permanently for *decades* now and guzzling millions of dollars a month. What is it doing but sowing discords between brothers (the Koreans)? And of course keeping high the defence budget? In this, the US is following Rome's downhill walk. She is inverting meanings of words to blackmail her citizens – hence the pervasive use of 'defending the stars-and-stripes' even when a drone is sent to hit another nation's Army in Aleppo. Rome was a master in wordplay. The end took her slowly, unaware.

Think this carefully: with a leading economy notwithstanding a majority citizens of the US are but living in 'hope'. They are the most taxed lot on earth. The government collects huge taxes through a well-knit tax net very few are ever shrewd to evade. Yet the tax isn't *in the main* constructing roads, railways, schools, hospitals and colleges. Of late, the tax is *majorly* buying fighter jets, missiles, tanks and an array of hand weapons – from private investors. Ones always looking to maximise their profits.

The Air Force is throwing billions of dollars to some private ventures to acquire *unusable* war technologies. Take the Lock Heed Martin's piece F22 Raptor Jet (the war monster pictured in the middle of this issue) at a price tag of USD 66 billion a piece. The USA had purchased 197 pieces by year 2011 (a far cry given the size of her Air Force and its scattered, tactical camping per the US futile idea of functioning global military bases). With that number alone one has got a glimpse at who grabs the lion's share of the US taxes.

The F22 Raptor is ahead of its era it isn't going to ply its trades in our time. When I say it is unusable and a waste I have evidences for that. But the best for you would be to review the debates on its acquisition. Distinguished arguments come from top brasses including Sen. John McCain (a warmonger who wanted nothing less for his country), the 17th Chairman of the Joint Chiefs of Staff Admiral Mike Mullen and then President Barack Obama and secretary of defence Robert Gates. The aforementioned entered in a war of words with the Congress, opposing irrational acquisition of those birds. The Congress was divided but what? The influential portion, the pro group, eventually won. This because the weapon industry in USA has no mercy. Obama then warned,

> *"To continue to procure additional F-22s would be to waste valuable resources that should be more usefully employed".*

Obama was saying this when the US had 187 F22s in 2009. Despite his fierce patriotism and broad knowledge of the US security needs Sen. McCain saw buying more F22s as an outlandish spending. He was strongly supported by Sen. Carl Levin, a democrat from Michigan. They lost the argument – though not to the better one. They lost to the lobbyists actually.

Well, billions more are going into space technologies and space researches. These again are fields that take money from the public to private investors. And are closely tied to the defence budget especially through NASA. Now, here you have explanation why clever civilians such as Elon Musk moved from businesses of civil nature to technologies allied with the defence cycles – founding Space X et al. These smart fellows know where the US taxes are going. And they chose to be in the receiving pack. They are billionaires now and they will always be. See?

Space technologies and space researches sound great yeah but are remotely connected to people's lives. Their future implication to the people's struggle is any one's guess. They can hardly resonate to a life of a citizen struggling to pay utility bills or threatened by standing mortgages.

Meanwhile unemployment is becoming the US's chronic disease. Social benefits are making people frustrated – leading amongst them, healthcare. One party offers an affordable health care (the ACA) another jumps in and deprives the people what they had. The US is a new kind of supremacy. One that piles roiling uncertainties to her people and then walk to run exotic errands.

Arguments by most analysts over facts of what life is in the US today eventually have the phrase 'nothing is certain'. There is no certainty in political decisions because politicians are wholesomely disconnected from the people. Temporary *economic* shifts dictate the shape, impetus, form and direction of decisions. The common citizens know very well that what is next for them is in the hands of those politicians. Although they also know the politicos must play foul. And they cannot predict what politicians think. Thus slowly but surely the US democracy has taken away the ability of her citizens to decide or take politicos to task. Sheer uncertainty rules... The words of Plato on 'the democratic man' in his book *"Republic"* are vindicated. Read Plato's condemnation of democracy in the later parts of this treatise.

Drudgery Is The Word

Like it was in the heydays of earlier civilizations so it is in the US today. People are thrown off economic tracks such that each passing day they grow confused and are prone to a changing policy/business environment. Again, there is the boiling citizenship crisis especially amongst immigrants. This gives tensions with far reaching consequences (I expound on this in the last part). Identities are already at issue. Economic policies keep changing ahead of people's conscience. Do you see? The American people have lives not worth their great value(s) even when they truly earn it.

Through a market system that excruciatingly takes each penny out of pockets, lives get twisted over and over by prevailing/fleeting interests. This is the work of intermittent economic/business environment regimes. Taxation is in perpetual fluidity whereas credit crunches beckon uncalled for. Blames have it that all these are deliberately engineered by political scammers working in some backrooms.

Well, I say, *naturally* large economies are full of contradictions...

So to live and move on common folks in the USA must possess working knuckles – red knuckles. Majority low classes are working two or more jobs to earn a decent living. The taxman beckons and takes a sizeable chip of the income hard earned working double. Then the Senate and Congress tirelessly *scheme* to deprive the poor of an affordable health care (Obama's ACA). An affordable heath care that was passed after spending outrageous sums. And a vexing time so to say. That is a master class of 'shylocking', uh! This relentless welfare insecurity means the people have to work all their lives to earn bread, get their bodies clothed and pay rents when it is due (and mortgages).

Say now, what do they have in common? Drudgery it is. The wealth of common citizens in an economy with disparities so high is drudgery.

One Treacherous Economy

Most analyses of dynamics in the US economy reveal that for great parts, people lead lives not as greener as outsiders are made to believe.

Despite an economy larger several times than combined GDPs of the next eight economies, Americans are insecure, desperate and mostly unhappy. It is a small population of industrialists that calls the future. This very economic *setup* means a majority cannot be happy. Psychologists know well why high economic disparities pre-empt happiness. It is because the majority become 'hoppers'.

They hop onto fleeting political-economic rafts. Nothing is to them ever certain. They are permanently revisited by surprises and indecisions. For example, the people do not decide the visceral parts of their lives or how tomorrow finds them. But they have to bear the blunt therefrom.

Literally speaking the US political economy is smarter it is way ahead of 'the people'. This chiefly because it is a compound of individualism, globalism, capital movements, corporate competitions and the changing global business environment – the market and all that. These aspects change from time to time. Thus, the economy leads the way – yes, leaving drudgery in its wake. The drivers of the US economy are externalities.

Americans toil *perhaps* the hardest on earth and do many jobs at a go to earn steady living. However, they cannot be sure what they have in the present will hold in the near future - let alone in the distant. This because a number of irregular political proclamations, new policies, frequent tax adjustments, an ever changing social benefits and legal ramifications theretofore send pre-existing household welfares slack and/or set in new arrangements. It is a flagging welfare status – and to cope one needs red knuckles.

Again the US economy is spiral. That says how difficult it is for a fledgling individual to cope.

Many recent reports (since year 2018+) from the department of labour, coupled with employment statistics by PR firms, cast a bleak picture of what is becoming of the US workmanship. Although figures show the economy going good – recovering and cutting unemployment stunts – analysts are nevertheless worried. Realities on the ground differ greatly from what is projected. There is one story on financial papers officially turned in, yet another in the main street.

Experts argue that the current US job packages are killing the formal labour, replacing it with some short-lived, 'unpensionable' and unguaranteed works. Many contend Americans are entering a phase of labouring too focused on the employers' benefits than the benefits of tenure. They point out how people are left with jobs less-valued compared to what used to mean 'employment' in the traditional perspectives. In short: the successful classes – the employers, the rich – are seen smoothly shirking employers' responsibilities. They are budding a new form of labour relations that create new crafts of surplus values. Values that make the rich shrewder and richer. Bargaining chip of all that is to give the people freedoms – some new freedoms they are growing pompous of.

Economics play tricks many a time...

Well, some seemingly good things are not purely good. Some of them are the modern technologies. Let me deliberately single out the lovely artificial intelligence (AI). AI is now popular in the US – the West at large – and is becoming globally preferable to human intelligence (HI). Innovators argue that an AI system does away with human clumsiness, misery and the burdensome conscience that is somehow irritating. For instance, an automated John Doe is cost-effective and is productive than human muscles will ever be. Better still Doe does not need expensive upkeep list of 'liabilities'.

What does that mean? It means this world is heading to a point in time the human sweat will be almost redundant and thus millions laid off – they are going to have nothing to do. This is to give room to economically viable AI. A brilliant idea if served with short-sightedness.

Yes with the fast growing use of AI, a steady loss of livelihood avenues for workers is underway. See?! The world is using sciences and technologies unconsciously than never before – *les sciences sans conscience*. If science keeps this unconsciousness going forward, a time is coming when all the people will sit back waiting on the machines (those employing the AI) to retire inventories of works accomplished. Does this sound bingo to you? I honestly hope it doesn't...

We cannot survive in a world where all our jobs are done by machines. For that would make us an idle mind and you know well an idle mind is the devil's workshop. It is unlikely we can still be around two centuries on.

It is universally proven that labour entails some degrees of 'sweating'. Hard labour more so and is very healthy. The straining of muscles, the rushing of blood and the warming of our brains that come with hard labour – hard thinking – are good for the tones of muscles and sharpness of our mind respectively. Manual labour helps man sweat, it pushes blood flows ahead and unmistakably consumes the calories that hail from the foods we eat. Labour consumes a chunk of body glucose that would otherwise dock there, poison the body.

With work *now* done in a poise of utter calmness and little or no scrabbling one doesn't sweat. There is no heat dynamics in the muscles rather there is gradual thinning of the veins. Science has brought a host of work sophisticating facilities. For all the goodness they are, science is again *disorienting* the natural functioning of human bodies. And now it is paving ways for total dependence on technologies. This is partly the reason successful people in developed economies are growing fragile health wise and/or are psychologically becoming expendable.

Living has made them too easy a life.

One can argue big time (or simply wave it off) but eventually one will come to terms with the fact that manual labour is a respected putter. Children who start out working relatively hard alongside their parents later grow sharper minds than those pampered and doted on.

Diseases prone to the body's own self – defending mechanism (and are a majority) get sorted out when one sweats considerably. All these are firm truths in life sciences and fitness education. With no natural room to work muscles – sweating while accomplishing a constructive notion – people are instead encouraged to sweat in gyms. A gym is a paid service. To do well at the gym one needs a good instructor. A good instructor who knows her stuffs is not a cheap broad! Thus 'gyming' equals an *economization* of sweat. How smart?! One pays for her own sweating.

America's Imperialism, Curse Of Patriotism

No word in Ages has had so many killed than 'patriotism'. Reflectively speaking, Americans' blood litter the world. Many have died at the beck and call of patriotic actions. Whether you went to Vietnam, Somalia, Afghanistan, Iraq, France, Germany and you mention others America's sons have had their blood sputtered. They were *in the main* innocents killed in what their state (only their state does) call 'patriotic wars'.

The heroism that America's history bequeaths her young generations doesn't, sadly, report millions of poor American souls wasted in different patriotic causes and doesn't pronounce why. Neither does it elevate hundreds of thousands mentally deranged. Nor does it soothe the number of crippled young men who have had their lives turned invalid. Many of them have had their lives clad in bitter memories. An only consolation they get is that they are 'war veterans'. That they were 'Patriots.' None of those words can take them to the banks. None can give them an own kid.

One won't believe it ever happens but is likely going to read it more often. A lady or a gentleman posts on a social network say, 'my father was a patriot who went forth to defend our rights in the Nam (she means Vietnam). He was a true American unlike Donnie (she means Donald Trump) who found ways to avoid call to duties. Dumbass Donnie'.

What is mind troubling here is that there still are millions of Americans (young generations sadly) out there who think wars of invasion to distant lands mean 'defending America's rights'. What rights, exactly? With this, one wonders how the US teaches her generations. She even denies them proper definition of events in their contextual sincerity. A war to topple a foreign leader (say Bashar al-Assad of Syria) is dabbed by American *'net-izens'* 'defending America's interests'. One misses Old Rome.

In several parts of this treatise I show that whatever America has built in the 'states' is a preserve of the moneyed. The wars, the sophisticated labour, the modern technologies and the patriotism so cherished by many end up serving a few private citizens owning leading sectors – industrialists and technologists mainly. Sectors that coach money and power.

All wars America masterminds boil down to profiteering. Weapons' sales and war diplomacies bring money – not peace at all. The right arm that carries the two is the 'weaponry department'. The latter's tentacles are the 'intelligence corps'.

The Centre Cannot Hold

It comes to pass that if one waves off the façades America's political *ulema* dress when arguing issues, there remains a perennial 'business of cheating' the public. The way it was done inside the Forum and Senate of ancient Rome so it is done in the American Congress and Senate. They debate issues heatedly only to end with decisions arrived at through 'games of numbers'. That is, issues that win the floor are not of, by and for the people but are of, by and for 'conspirators'. Members doing obscure, successful-party-schemes carry the day.

Some clandestine yet powerful alliances, networked mainly within the establishment and the military complex have the de facto trump seed to win what becomes of the USA.

It is surprising and elusive when one considers that at around 328 million (take or add a few tens), majority Americans are disconnected from the politics of their federation. Close examinations reveal that Americans are mostly unaware of the simplest political issues crushing them down.

Some years ago, for example, selected interviews at Universities in USA had 60% of sampled students unable to name the previous president. And more couldn't name who the current Secretary of State was. This despite the man having been one popular democrat, an ex-presidential candidate and Senator; John Kerry. Is this normal? Is this how things should be? No. It should not be that. But it happens. This is because preoccupation there is 'to earn a living'.

Say it aloud: TO EARN A LIVING is what prevails amongst the people of the largest, modern economy... What a marvel?

...in the Last Days of America's Hegemony (10)

In the USA presently politicos do 'games of numbers'. It would suit this part very well to say a bit about that game plan.

The game of numbers is not a democracy, but a charm inserted in what would have been a practice of popular politics. In the play, those who matter are the trump-seed (read: the Senate and the Congress) whereas the majority (the public) is a pawn. I just wrote the last sentence in more or less a parable. I must return to it.

On election of new faces to the Congress and the Senate, the establishment quickly identifies their men. These are politicians who align to the establishment's whims, ideas and personalities. Habituated politicos quietly tally the entrants. As the 'midterms' close they know who they have and who is lost. This is per rules of some esoteric set of virtues. Virtues based on lobbying and partisanships. This creates a number blocks hidden in the backrooms of democratic practice. The blocks are 'people who matter'. There are people who matter in this and people who are liabilities in that. Others are noted for meddling. Everyone's vote is important down the line because when circumstances call, they act to their number value. They are always relied upon and therefore they are the true swings used to cheat the public.

The majority block – the common voters who roam the main street – are pawns. One would think they are *albeit* remotely the ones words 'the walking sleepers' were meant for. They are powerless patriots, only they have abilities to parrot. They are regularly called upon to vote. But voting 'elections' is all they do. A clever form of false conscience it is. Given how sardonic America's democracy is, elections gorge sham practices called for every four years. And each consumes an earmarked stagger-ing sum of money. There is a constancy actually. One that involves public relations companies (lobbyists) making big cash each countdown to elections. If one examines that practice more closely all that comes up is a discovery that there is yet another money making plant. The idea is to throng the people to have their choices – candidates they wish – based on mere words/promises said at some rallies and throughout media engagements. With the vote casting practice perfected, the people presumably have had their ways...wow! Too simplistic you see. Well, political reasoning isn't that simple.

In short the majority *own* pompous votes.

Being pompous votes is evident when elected candidates form the pack. In the legislators' house, entrants find out: one, they need allies if only to influence anything. But lobbyists are on call around the clock (and they must have their ways) and there is an unrelenting climate of in-house tussling. Two, the fledglings come to a realisation that blackmailing, mudslinging, outsmarting, arm-twisting and whitewashing are the *truest* Houses' standing orders. But all these are hidden from what the public sees. Third, the novices to the house of legislation discover that the Congress votes in support of 'the influential' not the utility of tabled motions. And fourth, that the reins of lobbyists are tighter than the public scrutiny ever is. The last explains why novices/entrants are always brighter, raucous and dedicated at first. Likewise, it informs why the same soon get subsumed as they grapple with 'finding their places' in the House and its committees. That is America's true democracy at a glance.

The Us Democracy Is A Phantom

The history of democracies tell of attempts by the pioneers/ancient societies to create a 'utopia'. This was born of wishful idealism than some practical adaptations. They idealised bringing all the people at par with their leaders in all issues of decision making. That was basically a populism that could only be real in dreamlands. An ideal kind of leadership they wished, mmh! And they called it 'democracy' - from the old Greek's 'demos' which means people and 'kratia' which means 'leadership/rule'. The idea was to have 'a formal rule' wherein people were vocal and could determine their fate through the votes they regularly cast. A thought of immense grandeur, one would say. One that attacks the very human nature – of self-asserting.

Too good to be true.

The story of democracy is sad because sincerely, democracy was strangled the moment it was born. Then at each phase there always were malignant people to derail the wagon.

Whether you read the ancient Greek philosophers or the Roman orators after them you learn that at each moment democracies faltered as a result of the practitioners' reverting to some 'games of numbers'. The leading classes, for example in Athens and Rome, smartly bored holes in the voting practices. They erected safety nets for and against who could be inducted - when and how. They then sowed much freedoms (or illusion of rights, as *a matter of fact*) therein, freedoms through which *few* weasels got their ways. So democracies would eventually fall in the hands of the influential *Chichidodos* (the Orwellian killjoys, sort of) and get used to conduct *other* businesses. For this reason the ancient philosophers, Plato and Aristotle amongst them, decried democracy and refuted its practice calling it a blatant brainwashing of the mass. The two shouted themselves dry showing why games of cheating were done and the means used by shrewd politicians to get their ways. Democracy to them seemed no more than the chessboard game today, you see!

Since that classical period, philosophers have argued that the 'people's representatives' is in fact a wall (a farce) put in place to quell popular conscience. That the horde in 'the House' represents no one but themselves. The representatives are there to earn fat cheques and do some whimsical dilly-dallying. To show how this 'zombie culture' really works, I take liberty to discuss Plato's main illustration in the *Republic*. After that, I have to connect Plato's eyes to the US democracy. No democracy is 'whimsical' than America's.

Us Democratic Practices In The Eyes Of Plato

Plato, an intellectual in Athens, lived 428 – 347BC. He was a son of the Athenian political democracy who lived and felt it. He wasn't an outsider *really* for his father, Ariston, was *possibly* a courtier at the palace of Athens. Some *guess* his old man was a top judge. Whatever it comes to Plato grew and came of age surrounded by those who 'pulled' the reins of power. His father died when the son was young but he left him a legacy in the bloodline – they were from the lineage of nobilities of Athens, possibly including the great Solon, a reputed law-giver.

Plato grew hearing whispers of and saw conspiracies for power and could tell how wealth (the money, the *drachma*) cut deals. While the citizens of Athens shouted themselves dry for their *lovely* democracy, freedoms, representation and the so called people's decisions *perhaps* Plato would easily tell how each layer of decision had come about. I am drawing this from the Athenian tradition of those days that discouraged a father keeping secrets from his son. They believed, the life of a father was the life of a son. His step-father, Pyrilampes, must had seen to it. He had married Plato's mother, Perictione, after she got widowed and the old man was her uncle actually. The chance is he had to please her, including being nice to her baby son - Plato.

Pyrilampes was a hugely popular - rich politician and a heavyweight diplomat Athens could trust in for an ambassador to Persia. Again, Pyrilampes was a close friend and a confidante of the greatest democrat Athens ever had, Pericles.

With all likelihoods Plato had extensive contact and knowledge of the Athenian democracy. Plato also got the best education possible then. And the training received turned him into one of the finest philosophers of politics. Some writers say philosophising became his decision after he realised that the democracy Athenians held high was actually treacherous and purely immoral. Whatever he saw and learned, we know Plato eventually got wholesomely uninterested with democracy. He in effect walked away from the juicy political opportunities that lay before him. This is what he saw and wrote...

On the source of democracy: Democracy came from a generation of ambitious sons of the top, domineering class known as the 'oligarchy'. So he observed that democracy is essentially a reactionary adaptation i.e. the oligarchic sons responded cleverly to the needs of time as a way to outsmart public sentiments. Thus, the origin of democracy is not the citizen. But the oligarchies moved to create a system wherein people would be left doodling/fooling with some ineffectual dreams and grandeur of freedoms which actually mean nothing *significant*. The clever fellows (the oligarchies) made 'freedom' of the people the presumed 'supreme good, proof of virtues'. But according to Plato – contrary to many critics today – it is 'freedom' that in a democracy forges 'slavery' of the people. He shows how in a democracy:

a)   People exercise 'their powers' but only through a voting scheme – this is a scheme they don't put in place.

b)   With such a scheme, the lower classes grow bigger and bigger to outgrow the true façade of power (which means the true power is made invisible).

c)   The poor, armed with the votes, become the winners – or so they think.

d)   With their perceived power over the top classes, the poor are free to do what they want, live how they want and enjoy it.

e)   And given the human nature (and the limitations a human has when doing freedom) the people can break laws if they choose (*reread this careful*)

f)   With abilities to break the laws and snub traditions the people create 'anarchy' – In anarchy people do violations of rules (*as born from their limitations*).

g)   It is at this point that the democratic man sets into aid (*the clever fellows become saints – choose laws and decide life*).

But the democratic man, Plato says, has two desires: unnecessary and necessary desires. Unnecessary desires encompass those that are worldly and that one can resist if one chooses to. For example the love of riches, coveting powers, decadent life styles and egoistic manipulations. Sadly, this line of desires appeal more to the human nature and are difficult to handle. Necessary desires are those we have by instinct i.e. ones we have for survival e.g. desire for foods, sex, comfort etc. The democratic man is consumed by the unnecessary desires. For example, interest in all things he can buy with his riches, his money become more important than helping people and the nasty of all is he does whatever he wants whenever he wants. To that end, the democratic man's life has no order, necessity or priority (in my analyses in this treatise I show how this is the primary ethics of the US democracy: *no order, no necessity* and *no priority*).

With that textural exegesis in mind you see America's democracy is trading a phantom. It is a game that brings 'rats' to the leagues of 'cats'. The people in USA and the world at large are practicing an old tradition that allows camps in Congress and Senate – camps with 'alliances of whims' – to decide cabal, private motives in the name of the people (yet those decisions cannot take an order, a necessity or priority). Hidden somewhere between the rats and cats are the money-baggers (the filthy rich). In Plato's words, they are the 'drones'. All that the latter do is inciting the peoples' lives however they like, to encourage lawlessness (anarchy, see all those immoral laws the US is pushing the world to adapt) and this increase pressure on the democratic man (the state). The drones, Plato shows, have all the good people at their mercy and often 'kill' (destroy) them through this or that trick to avoid good men's impact on the society at large.

While he lived, Plato saw many good men wasted and all they had done wrong was being sincere and/or trying to show the public that the mass were being made fools by the democrats. One distinguished most of good men whose life had influenced

Plato was the sage Socrates – the greatest moralist, teacher and philosopher of his time. The democratic sect of Sophists were dominant in Athens when Socrates taught people how to argue, reason, seek truth and take the Sophists to the basics. The democrats couldn't match Socrates – his goodness was transcendental and awed many, spreading far and wide. The Sophists tried all they could to win his followers but the latter kept staunchly stubborn. Socrates soon suffered trumped-up charges and accusations far-fetched. He was condemned to die from a cup of poison. They got rid of him that way – sending a strong message to his likes and his students.

Many a good men suffered similar fate.

Actually, in a grown-up democracy it is *very* risky for just men to tell the truth – because the drones have a loop called *McCarthyism* to hang the down-to-earth. Or simply purge them of their elements.

The history of US democracy has very clear and uncontested examples of good men wasted in the same way. Presidents: Abraham Lincoln and John F. Kennedy were mortally shot to nip their impact on the larger society. The pacifist-preacher, civil rights activist Martin Luther King is another one of many. Character assassination is so rampant that politicians and the mainstream media do them on daily bases – on behalf of patrons hiding in the shades.

In the USA the drones have an extra, tricky 'clique' known as the lobbyists. Lobbyists (the cotter pins of the Western democracy) do fast-tracked adoption of agendas, soiling the good men, laying sinister schemes and enabling dirty money to change hands – far and wide. These PR lieutenants essentially have a hell of lucrative businesses tossing billions of dollars around.

The drones are money fingers. The politicians (democrats and republicans in USA) need to exercise power. The people need freedoms. See, in USA today, the people's freedoms are tipping towards anarchy. They demand homosexuality and they have it. If they want 'weeds' to smoke their brains 'haywire' they have that – legally, burn the lungs it's your life. They need abortions, well, slay 'em all foetuses. If it is divorce and/or contractual marriage – well, take as many spouses as you want, but each at a time. One doesn't need home his old parents? Yeah, throw 'em in a care home – forget the old folks' nuisance. Guns in one's house? Well, buy as many as you want, make your arsenal – and the state will care less if you kill each other like pigs. A person can sin against the state: kill, rape, steal or do anything but if one has something to trade to the democratic man – say secrets – one is assured of leniency. Or, a walk scot-free.

Have you ever heard the story of Gary Ridgway, 'the green river killer'? He sinned abhorrently: killing humans, raping corpses! He fucked putrefying bodies really. But he had something to trade for his life against the tens of lives (they are estimated to be about 70 women) he had sent to early graves. He had secrets for buying leniency. He is enjoying his full life in public houses paid for by the states (prisons). Sad. There are hundreds or thousands of similar decisions each year country-wide. It is called a plea bargain. It is business. Plato shows that this set of freedoms must exist because in the end they bring money to the drones. That is exactly what it is in USA. The correctional facilities (the prison systems) are netting billions of dollars a year. Money that go to the wealthy.

Again, the more confused the people's lives are made the easier it becomes to manipulate them. Bob Marley says, it becomes easier to force 'them' into the devil's illusion. Justice is one such a useful handle to bring in handy confusion. How controversial!? They have a kind of arrangement that makes the laws 'potentially' redundant 'if...'

Plato again notes that to distract the people from realising that their freedoms are in reality enslaving them, the democratic man wage wars... wars everywhere. For in wars, the 'drones' recycle the ideas of patriotism, pride in a country's power and achieve all a country needs to sharpen her status amongst the nations. War is a renewal. Blackmailing it is.

The democratic state go on like that – people continue getting slowly eaten by their freedoms. Until there is no way out.

Each freedom brings money in the pockets of the drones. But the same freedoms eventually become sources of terrible social decadence, slavery of men and the reign of deplorable immorality. Freedoms displace beliefs, the gods, order, self-respect and the people's traditions. Say, things fall apart.

The ensuing immorality at this point cannot be stopped. Such life is the maker of an intolerable anarchy that groom tyrants. And so ends democracies – Plato concludes.

History says Plato was/is right. It is excessive freedoms that have all along the Ages shepherded the gutting down of democracies.

America Outdoing Herself

In USA a population of around 5% has the economy, available powers and resources working for them. That is Plato's drones. The majority doesn't have helms to drive the fate of their lives (as seen in the way democracy is practiced, the bargaining chip being freedoms even when they smoke the people's heads dry). Where they own properties the people pay exorbitant revenues to validate such ownership. Actually the collection goes to scaffold the wealthy (the drones). For example, the taxpayers have their taxes bailing out wealthy conglomerates and/or subsidising corporate interests in time of hardships, without popular consent. That is the poor paying to save the rich.

Yet there is systemic violence in the economy, credit system, laws and services throwing a majority off tracks each moment (another form of violence). Consumer safety is entirely whacked down the public can be treated with 'obsolete commodities' without suspecting. So the majority has eyes but do not see they are in a system wherein wielders of power keep throwing the public in the jaws of uncertainty. Drudgery is the order of the day. And thus the wider population lives in strange forms of economic, social, moral, technological and political fluidity. Household struggles of the day often end up with 'earning a living'. This last isn't what a progressing hegemon is based on... unless it is a waning one.

Outdoing herself in her last days is for an Empire a necessary path. There are solid records for this in almost all gone civilizations. Stages arrive in which powers oppose the very values that brought their polities' founders together e.g. traditions, religion, identities, history, the spirit of commonwealth, community power structure, cultural and moral codices etc. If you cannot see America is already there, think it over. For one, the quality of America's democracy today is downgrading such that it is ripe for tyranny. There are others, read on. Review the histories of ancient empires or brace for the next parts of this treatise. I've got something for you...

SECTION FOUR: **SEEDS OF DESTRUCTION**

...in the Last Days of America's Hegemony (11)

"The world must be made safe for democracy". These are the words America put forward when entering the global politics in the year 1917. This (as amply introduced in part three) was declared when Woodrow Wilson commanded the US Army to engage the Allied Powers and crush Germany.

I insist this: it was in the First World War – wherein people were indiscriminately doing the dying – that America commanded her hallowed democracy taken by the world.

The noble US democracy sank her deep roots in a life time of war. Keep your records sharp: the First World War is the deadliest conflict ever happened in human history. It wiped out more than 40 million in human lives – creating millions more cripples and injuries. It threatened to turn the earth into a planet home of abysmal poverty. With all that downfall of reason, America said the world needed democracy more than all others.

If anything, the timing chosen by the US is thought provoking. That when the world was in a frenzy of carnage, millions going unaccounted for, families going apart, economies shattering, refugees scurrying everywhere, poverty raging and this planet on blink of destruction America loudly jingled democracy – her prime item of sale. A sale to be made to a restive world. How strange America is!

They say times carry meanings. Well, America's timing for entry into global competitions is worth some academic endeavours.

I guess America believes in the astrological cycles of moon waxing and waning.

Read: 'when they are weak, strike'!

Entering the war she did, and because other powers were being torn and in shambles (weak/were waning) the US emerged leader of the victors. With only her power an edge above the rest (waxing). It was boom. Boon. As it would become, the hegemon America now is started with the millions of souls wiped out. One thinks blood sacrifice. At the climax of warring, America remained the only power with semblance of strong, working institutions e.g. the military, civil, economic and diplomatic organisations. She headed the West (and the world for that matter) in every respect – even the abilities to kill people. A journey had started – a journey towards the America and democracy Woodrow had in mind.

Here we are.

The True Maker Of America's Greatness Is Woodrow Wilson

We read history differently. And perhaps it better be that. For me, when it comes to reading America's history of predominance, I am one of those who believe the greatness of USA hinges on Woodrow Wilson as a statesman. The ideas, aspirations and works of President Woodrow (1913 – 1921) seem to have hibernated and almost got lost on the table when he was crafting them. Yet they sprang up wistfully as the man started festering in his grave at the Washington National Cathedral. In his days, he had tried to implement some ideas but failed considerably. That was not the end. A decade after he died America would turn Wilsonian in all her ideas and deeds.

America's belligerence, the fortitude, the cunning, the dreaming, the individualism etc. are wholly Wilsonian. His idealism *especially* and his craftiness in separating politics from public administration are what would spring up and rule America and the world. And are all thriving today. It would seem that the US's greatest of statesmen is the not so often spoken Woodrow Wilson. As a historian and someone always moved with intriguing coincidences, I must write a bit about Wilson's precarious presidency.

The Rejected, Shredded Dreamer... Won In Death.

America didn't welcome her brilliantly educated son when he chose to serve her. The 28th President, Woodrow Wilson, was an ex-college professor with immense record as a trainer and a top-notch PhD researcher. He is a man who left college(s) to go make his research theses in international relations, public administration and diplomacy practicable. Having been well educated, carrying gubernatorial experience and with enough competence in political science, he would eventually secure nomination of the Democratic Party. He became its flag bearer in the elections of 1912. It was from that very year's campaigns that he became a 'Donald Trump'. For a start he reneged most of his party's policies and abandoned the 'conservatism' that had seen his party pick him for the job. He instead declared and became leader of what he called a "progressive movement". The backlash to this snub became immediately felt inside his party. He had dared bite the hand that fed him... he would regret.

Like Trump's one man show against own Party's stance would hit back in 2016, Woodrow soon met a hard political terrain. He was an outsider and remarkably professorial. He was not of the establishment and therefore he wasn't favoured by the Washington cycles. He polled poor and in the elections of 1912 he lost popular votes (he got only 42%). He won instead by snatching more electoral colleges. His luck being that the election was three ways - for the Republicans had been torn into two parties. The win brought anger outburst. The system of electoral colleges became a vexing issue – the diehards frowned. The Republicans hated him outright and made a case to make things harder for him in his entire presidency. They would eventually 'sort of' kill him.

But before they destroy him Woodrow had shuffled his cards very well. He had few tricks rolled up his sleeves. The John Hopkins University professor had many years before 1912, the year he got nominated as presidential candidate, dreamt what he wanted for America. And he had written a lot about that. Woodrow had taught those dreams to hundreds of students and had audited his ideas over time. After disowning his party's conservatives and the machinery that had appointed him, he asserted his independence of partisanships. He had rightly thought that Party conservatism would grind his innovations so he declared and campaigned for "New Freedoms" insisting "individualism, trade tariffs and State's rights". He expected the three would appeal to the voters. The Senate and Congress would as usual try to limit him somehow but he had planned to outsmart the two by declaring to the public that "no one but the president seems to be expected to look out for the general interests of the country". Within that, his was an idea that in the case of representativeness, "only the president was the personal representative of the people". He fared through. From there he moved on, always outmanoeuvring the Congress to get his way.

Woodrow used a lot of means to outdo the Congress, for example, he wooed the public through a raft of legislations that favoured the poor against employers (a populism). His new freedoms grew sweeter. Individualism took faster paces and the state's rights got reshaped (reread Plato's analysis in the previous part on the state's rights). And when the people were almost dumping him in the 1916 elections Woodrow wagered for his re-election by popularising "he kept us out of war". The unsuspecting public voted him in again for the reason of not having taken them to the menacing state of war. Remember at this time the WWI was on rampage. Wow! But he was cheating. Woodrow threw Americans heads on into the First World War few months after he got sworn in (April, 1917). Fighting the war had been right in his all-time agenda and he regarded war as a very creative means for building a hegemon. According to one White House's own post on Woodrow, the Virginia born Princeton University graduate had in his young life seen the 'fruitfulness' of war. So he could never stand by and watch as the First World War raged on. He knew war is that rare occasion used to manoeuvre the people. See? Plato is right. A democracy cannot keep out of wars for long. Wars are periods of renewal and reaffirmation of the people's strength. Wars trade the notion of 'patriotism'.

Having outsmarted the Congress to drag the US to the First World War, the Virginia law school alumnus had his dreams to spread America's values (democracy, individualism and new freedoms amongst others) set in motion. His idealism was this far going to plan. The world had been trapped and he knew it. But he had a last bold stroke to make. One hurdle to jump. He had made Europe servile already and so he would act – and that ASAP! It was too easy. He wrote his notes/ideas actually, and boarded a plane to Paris one afternoon of early 1919. There he submitted his last trap in what is now famous to historians, political scientists and diplomats as "the Peace Treaty of Versailles ". Woodrow's 14 points of the treaty if taken would convert the world into America's own playfield. This of course coupled with the values he had built in USA during his presidency. The treaty would unavoidably give birth to a durable America's foreign policy environment. When he tabled the points, the world swallowed the bait and he went home smiling.

Only to be backstabbed by the Congress and die a horrifying death. "His kinsmen do not honour the…?" – Jesus is right.

It had happened that in the previous year's midterms – congressional elections of 1918 – his rivals, the Republicans, had gained control of the house. The game of numbers was thus not in the Virginia statesman's courtyard. The Republicans used their numbers as an opportunity to strike blows to the president's heart. He had played smart too long, now that they had the votes that mattered! They rejected to ratify the Versailles Peace Clauses and the President had no way out. He was in for the Nobel Peace Prize win following his moves, especially initiating the idea of the League of Nations, how dare the Congress be unthankful? So much for president as the sole representative of the people! His professor's head dealt Woodrow heavy blows when he thought (read: fell back to the idealism of democracy as people's power) he could still get his way by soliciting direct public sentiment. Against good advices of his doctors (he already had pre-existing health issues), the president made a nation wide tour to mobilize sentiments for the treaty. Fragile though he was. In that trip he got utterly exhausted and coupled with panic, the President suffered a stroke that almost immediately sent him to the graves. He held on to dear life though. But the complications therefrom would worsen over time. And they killed him in 1924. That is three years after leaving power.

Why have I taken space to show that Woodrow's centrality in what the US is today remains unmatched? It is because one cannot understand how Europe and the world fell preys to America's interest classes and political predation without reviewing Woodrow's intentions. He is the professor who left Princeton University lecture theatres to go harness his classroom ideas. His individualism, democratic freedoms (he called them new freedoms), state's rights and 'president as a personal representative of the people' are all what sprang up, rowed the US and are today killing America's long held traditions. America's neo-liberalism for example is an offshoot of Woodrow's individualism. And the so called new freedoms are mothers and guardians to US's current moral degeneration. The Versailles Peace Treaty's fourteen points are responsible for the present global arrangements. Hence this America's imperial peace and tranquility (the PAX AMERICANA) the world is in today.

He won.

Woodrow's Democracy Re-Considered

But what democracy is America's? America's democracy is a phantom. It is a democracy that has been dying at the hands of tyrants and getting resurrected by the oligarchies, all over the ages. I had an extensive argument on this in the immediate previous part. America's democracy is a rule (*through intrigues*) of the people, by the people and for the people. The trouble with America's democracy (as I elucidate here) is that the words 'the people' do not carry similar meanings in each of: of the people, for the people and by the people. In the de facto processes, votes that matter are cast *on real issues* by the Senate and Congress. Not the populace. And in the setup the drones prey on either votes. Thus there is: the public, the Congress and Senate and the moneyed drones. These are the different 'the people' Lincoln's words refer to. This is a natural flaw in all representative democracies though. 'Representativeness' is a farce. It never exists. At staggering sums of money – billions of dollars – Americans get paraded every four years to vote for representatives 'who convinced them' on campaign trails'. As I stated in part ten of this volume, these elected representatives end up playing/getting played on 'games of numbers'. They are 'invitees' of the lobbyists. Guests of the drones – the lazy male bees. All the 'hosts' know well is sting and impregnate. The whole democratic practice is thus full of theatrics. America's democracy is complex than a majority believe. Might as well be incomprehensible.

America's Democracy Is A Dracula

Evident is that spreading America's democratic practices have led to grim bloodshed. At the onset, America had to fight wars to get proper footing for her endeared democracy. Wars that included and followed World War I & II. A lot of kingdoms and dictatorships in Asia, Latin America and Africa got flipped upside-down. Later, wherever America's democracy wasn't favoured the US carried attacks against that place's existing social rubrics. For example, she either set up violent proxies, engineered regional disparities, orchestrated civil strifes, spoiled integrities of nations or couched 'balkanisation'. A proper count should tally hundreds civil wars globally. The last being strifes inundated with bloodletting – first conceived by the US intelligences.

Nations-other have paid prices too high to buy America's democracy of intrigues. Costs involve but are not limited to: propensity of bloodbath amongst vying factions and inferiority complexity amongst foreign leaders, majority of whom have to *worship* the White House to retain power. Furthermore, many nations abandoned their pre-existing socio-political 'decorum' and there is perpetual insecurity amongst less favoured politicians in the third world countries. There is a *skewed* internationalisation of political space. It is a democracy that has depraved the imitators (or adoptors?) the possible policy environment they would have had, had they been in their own crafts of leadership. It pits 'rats and cats'. The last is exactly what Woodrow Wilson dreamt of in his idealism – "the world must be made safe for democracy". Democracy was in 1917 in America's own manners and prism *thus* 'the world must be made safe for America' is what he really meant.

America's democracy knows no border separating morality and immorality – the common citizen may not be suspecting this but that is it. It remains anarchic as long as money is involved. For example, the elites advocate a host of 'liberal rights' even when the same subset of cultural introductions do insult the common goods long known of America and humanity. This mind-set was partly responsible for legalisation of homosexuality and now *ganja*. Their democracy doesn't care whatever. If the so called neoliberal cultural traits can bring money, immoralities are declared moral. You see? There is a joke somewhere law experts are entertaining. It being that 'morals' are so important that a society cannot live without them – the laws cannot take the place of morals either. Then both morals and laws are not held because they are right, no. It is because they serve some practical purposes that they were made or adopted. Some morals and laws *in many societies* are so merciless they are counterproductive yet they aren't just thrown away. This is because their other impact is great in many 'other' respects apart from the obvious. The USA is trying to 'unlearn' this fact - and is pushing other nations to that corner as well. That is the joke.

Again, think this: Americans do elect representatives to the Congress to say in the name of the people. Very bright idea. In a working democracy of the US calibre where do they extract the role of 'lobbyists'? In practice lobbyists are professional *schemers.* They are 'crooks' who buy and snatch the people's representatives. To what end? Racketeering – one should presume. Or it draws down to that. There in dies the US democracy...

America's democracy doesn't call a spade a spade. They don't say frankly that the PR (lobbying) moles are embedded vote fraudsters. But they are. They are clever outfits that swing decisions to causes far removed from the public. The lobbyists are an intelligence unit for all they do. They share their central methods and execution of plans with the likes of the CIA, FBI and NSA. That is, they work around the clock to gather and synthesize information they use to conflate courses of events (just like any other standard intelligence agency). This is a big, regrettable weakness the US founding fathers didn't know would come. It has outsmarted the common folks.

Core Values Under Attacks

America's vast academics: psychologists, sociologists, historians and the whole intellectual bodies are dancing to a tune of time. They are lying all is well but they know better. America is outdoing herself. They see beyond doubt that the core values the US used to espouse are downtrodden to dust by an increasing, ever nagging irrational liberalisation. See, churches – institutions with long held, time-tested and proven morals, noble traditions – are *now* totted as wrong, inferior and hoaxes. Millions of Americans are *ashamed* of being identified *devote* Christians. The internet is awash with denigration of the faith, God, Christian morality, Christian upbringing etc. A Christian American is despised worse than is a believer of religions coming to America more recently: Buddhism, Hinduism, Islam, etc. America's young generations are instead parading some scientific theories they hope will replace 'godhead' and uphold *atheism*. It is a clear shift from the traditions that have worked for them all over the ages. Their central argument is that they are educated better than their foolish grandfathers. Now for the first time in history the earth has a well learned society that is willing to hop onto and believe in theories (evolution and atheism) that haven't proven a thing beyond having some 'generalizable' assumptions.

But what led to the rise of America in the first place? Which orientation did America's conscience, life and nationhood pursue and hold steadfastly in all its tempests? Well, it is/was there on the Great Seal. A firm belief that declares "IN GOD WE TRUST". America was born out of the womb of a Christian lady. But today the wising-up 'gentlemen' are *ashamed* of their old mom. Movements are growing to demand the words 'In God We Trust' washed off. So far the words are being attacked as irrelevant to stand as US's motto. Some *geniuses* are arguing the words aren't reflective of what the US now is. According to them America is *now* greater than God. As big as atheism America is - they think.

Again, the wave to bless same sex cohabitation through the churches' formality is striking hard. Even pushing too hard to have churches (well-known conservative institutions) to tie knots between such '*sexers*'. Which means those who want sodomy are receiving better attention than those who think it is wrong – the likes of Churches, Synagogues and Mosques. They don't remember: an insult to one's right is an insult to all. Insulting and picking on those institutions will in the end dishonour whatever will replace them.

Again equality of men and women, however palatable that sounds, is accelerating bitter forms of parenting. This is public knowledge. Father absence destroys a people – the black community of USA has been there, they can bear witness. Mother absence ruins a nation – there are groups in UK now evaluating this and are shouting big warning. The two developments are bitter and destructive. This last no one sane can argue against. Those parenting approaches are settling in new psychosocial dimensions difficult for the society to handle.

This far the West is pushing for evolution of 'scientifically judged' social values and intimacy. A very wrong move indeed. Everyone knows mankind isn't a scientific being. We are social beings, full stop. This explains why from the very cradle of civilizations (when Babylon's Hammurabi penned the Lex Talionis) science didn't dictate values, the society did. And the society made laws with all biases. So, laws are not that much just (right) and they shouldn't be – lest we all end in prisons. Or kill ourselves.

Whilst decisions are made by politicians competing in games of numbers, America's population is torn between the phantoms of academic utopia and struggling/waning traditional values. It is evident in ways more than one that majority 'down-to-earth' Americans are desperate. For example, an American aging parent finds/reckons he cannot get attention of his adult children and so he has to live in a 'care house' to wind up. One's children are no longer her eventual caregivers to see her off life. What a time!

A responsible father who seared and reared sons hoping they would one day make grandchildren in the clan's name – as a course of nature – learns that laws for homosexuality may snatch his son(s) for a seductive homo. It is frustrating. More so because this freedom forecloses what one can forge his boys into. Say, a foreclosure of the parents' role in their children's future. A very wrong footing in all measures.

If that closure was pushed onto Barbara Bush when she was raising her children, certainly she would have been horrified. Many reporters, biographers, family friends and commentators alike identified Barbara as a no nonsense lady who took parenting to heart. She asserted herself in the views of her children. She allowed no compromise and she was the brain behind her successful family – directing and masterminding the young Bushes with resolve and chosen ends in sight. Barbara enlivened her influence in the children's world views and tolerated no slow learning. Well, here I am saying the lady responsible for upbringing George, Jeb, Dorothy, Pauline, Neil and Marvin Bush. They grew to become a fortified, respected lot. Yeah, that is what parenting is. What else is a parent for if not 'forerunning' to set paths for his/her children? Aren't humans better than hens? No law should foreclose that.

Some scientists out there are arguing men do not have finite sexual roles. Roles are infinite – they claim. And they are saying sexes are infinite. What a world, uh! Well, if so, providence did overlook one important sense. That in the end, biological construction is going to mean nothing. It is going to seem terribly unfair. One day someone is going to take his boy to a maternity clinic – when the boy is pregnant, mmh! As long as you say 'sex' isn't anything finite but an orientation, you cannot rule out possibility that boys will one day be 'oriented' to conceive and give birth to pretty girls. And when it happens, it will be unfair because then men will be having double privileges. They will be able to play father and mother at a go. This means female redundancy. I wouldn't choose to be alive in a world where women are so relegated.

Whether that claim hails from much knowing (an illusion of knowledge) or some social adventurism, we learn America's outlook is stuck in anarchy and is wandering therein. She is eroding her once *very* efficient values. Values that put her people together in the first place. The sanctity of family and the blissful bed-time communion between a man and a woman being some of them. And in this instance the world has America's neoliberal democracy to blame... It has reduced very complex biological constructions into mere *'orientations'*... and the earth has had to live through *those* hypothetical ideas... A civilization cannot sustain on hypotheses...

Wh en their hegemonies last empires sink deep in machtpolitik that they idolise themselves being better than any other political, social and economic entities that went before them.

At the peak empires think they are better than humanity itself. This is one of the many reasons they trample on life and waste lives to serve illusions.

At extreme points – which are marked by exceeding comforts, love of worldly pleasures, human shamelessness and arrogance of higher levels and, of course, mercurial bullshit trends – civilizations attempt separating humanity from nature (distorting the known based on half-baked truths) and dare wage war(s) against God/gods. The most known ill fates of civilizations have been recorded starting from the time men wage war(s) against gods (beliefs). And this begin the time men think they are too knowledgeable to be contained by mere beliefs or some traditions from the dead/old generations (it's known as narcissism). That they no longer need a god. That they are better than their gone forefathers. That they have knowledge and that is enough. That is a costly mistake born of overlooking. Let us entertain one view...

Lo Narrates

> *The oldest stories ever told are written in the stars. Stories of time before man and gods, when the titans ruled the earth. The titans were powerful but their reign was ended by their own sons: Zeus, Poseidon and Hades. Zeus convinced his brother Hades to create a beast so strong it could defeat their parents. And from his own fresh, Hades*

gave birth to an unspeakable horror: the Kraken. Zeus became king of the heavens, Poseidon king of the Seas and Hades, tricked by Zeus, was left to rule the Underworld in darkness and in misery. It was Zeus who made man and man's prayers fed the gods' immortality. But in time, mankind grew restless. They began to question the gods and finally rise up against them. In this world, a child was born. A boy who would change everything.

The Narratives And Mankind

The narratives Lo offers in the motion picture "Clash of Titans" are recycled stories from different societies of the ancient world. This Greek version is a story of Perseus, the half human half god son of Zeus. The ancient narratives are digests that pre- and-postdate the Greek mythologies amongst which the story of Perseus hail. They present some world views that *somehow* were responsible for the making of almost all modern, global religions. For example, the story of emanation is there – being that, the Titans were the oldest, powerful rulers of the universe through whom everything started. Then the Titans would be dethroned and get totally destroyed by their *own* sons the gods: Zeus, Poseidon and Hades. To the pantheon's joy the *higher* god Zeus would create mankind to worship them, and man's prayers feed the gods' immortality. To their chagrin, man would *in time* grow powerful and restless as to wage war(s) against the gods. That is, every champion falls to his own records. The *tricky* part of that story is that 'mankind couldn't win a war against the gods standing pure mortals'. Until a son was born, a boy of a higher god (Zeus' boy son). A son of a god. A half god, half man was required to overrun the Olympians.

The story is very interesting despite its original agenda, as per the movie's bold daring, having been propagation of aggressive *atheism*. It is thought provoking especially because the producers and directors do (?perhaps inadvertently) scale their thoughts. It has countless angles but see this, the powerful titans are fallen by their own sons. And those boys no longer are titans – rather, gods. How do the gods successfully subdue their powerful parents (the titans)? Through their own creation it is. The gods' own offspring. That is, an elemental beast – the Kraken – is made by Hades from his own parts. He calls it his child – and it is powerful enough to thwart the primordial titans. The story again shows the gods, with all their powers, being *in time* outfought (?sort of payday) by the mortals. The mortals (mankind) become powerful before they grow restless enough to confront their immortal creators. Of course that happens after the mortals have received an aid from Perseus – a son of god. According to that story therefore the gods (through the head of the pantheon – Zeus – laid the foundation for their own downfall).

Another scale hidden in there is that the evolution (or is it a shift?) from Titans → gods → mankind is *reductio ad absurdum*. That is, it is reduction to absurdity. Say, one powerful, intelligent generation is outsmarted/outmuscled by the next poor, less powerful, intelligent generation down the line (incredible, wouldn't you say?). So the powerfulness, intelligence of the original beings keep dwindling through the Ages. Mankind, the weakest being in the chain takes his era through successful violence against the gods (his rather more powerful, intelligent makers). We see the gods eventually fall to the feet of their own creation. See?! The whole myth is about power and is *reductio*. What it gets better than most stories ever told is the underlying revelation (?a warning maybe) that as per 'essence of beings' life is moving from strength to weaknesses – from intelligence to negligence. That on the racecourse of strife, the weak have been winning the race.

Well, what about mankind, the last in the chain that far? Has man ever created any one, anything? Anything seemingly weaker to him? Yes. Mankind has created a lot. Many of them after crashing and exerting himself such that they are part of his body and mind. Is man going to kneel down (to be overpowered by) at the feet of his own creation? The technologies, the sciences, the megalomaniac ideas, the mind-wiring philosophies and the material wealth he is absurdly accumulating. This inquiry is interesting indeed. Looking at how careless, self-depraving and self-enslaving mankind is using those offshoots of his creativity the answer is clear. Mankind will in the end be destroyed by his own making. No society represents the clarity better than does the USA. She is the head-strong player of the offshoots. She is destroying herself at an alarming rate. She is matter-of-factly already held hostage by them...

The story of Perseus is in itself a chip of the story of the biblical Moses floating on the waters of Nile in a chest/basket of reeds. Yet it again is the story of Jesus son of God, born of Mary – a virgin impregnated in ways so mysterious. While Jesus' story is younger than Perseus', Perseus' story is contemporary to Moses'.

The story of the Olympian wars between men and gods is told by the ancient Greek 'mythographers' around the 9th or 8th century BC. They tell it as a tale of an old era far gone, we can thus assume it is dated far back as to be close to the ages Moses is said to have lived (around 2,000 years BC). Well, all those stories are younger in comparison to the original texts of stories of this nature – a half god, half man coming to influence and aid humanity. Or, stories of a strange boy floating in a basket of reeds somewhere. The story could be contemporary to another narrative of a floating big ship escaping a cataclysmic deluge. A ship made to serve mankind and a host of species. The Hebrews found a name for it – it's Noah's Ark. The Ark on the other hand is as old as the Epics of Gilgamesh written in the fourth millennium BC. The Gilgamesh narratives, perhaps the oldest stories ever written by man, are Mesopotamian. They date to the days of mighty Uruk – the seat of the oldest pantheon known.

Uruk was a big city that bordered and once ruled Ur. Ur, another Mesopotamian city-state, was the Chaldeans' capital whose patron deity was the moon god Nanna. Nanna was a god highly regarded and named variably in the wider Mesopotamia e.g. Sin, Suen, Namrasit and other *localised* names were used to refer to him. He was a god celebrated and worshipped based on the calendar of the lunar cycle – the waxing and waning of the moon – throughout the year. Therefore he is known as the god of moon and wisdom. His symbol is the bull's horn, amongst others – the horns being the closest physical resemblance to a crescent moon.

But Nanna wasn't the overall god of Mesopotamia, he was at first a mere patron deity of Ur, a son (first born) of Enlil and Ninlil. He had a wife, Ningal, and several children. His seat in the south of the Fertile Crescent was Ur but he also was worshipped in Harran, another Semitic city to the north in the large fertile field known as Paddan Aram (the field of Aram). The two, Ur and Harran, are the lands where came a well-known patriarch of the Hebrews (later the Jews). A man who is the seed of Judaism, Christianity and Islam. His name is Abram/Abraham. As per Jewish traditions that have come down to us, Abraham left Ur sometimes in the Bronze Age. That is, around 3200 BC. This date is predated by the stories of Gilgamesh and the great upheavals amongst the gods of ancient Mesopotamia.

It is within Abrahamic religions wherein the lesson of a God who is the ultimate source of emanation starts. One God. Anything ringing an alarm bell in your? There should be a loud one. That alarm is nothing but an eye opener that should tell you humanity has all along seen continuity and is driven by love of mysteries. The lessons are clear though. Amongst them that: 'beings' have been destroying themselves over the ages. At least that is how the ancients saw life. They saw strife and tried to define it – hence they invented the gods and found ways to place mankind at the helm of all that the gods could do. The gods became creators and vanquishers of mankind, yet ones who depended on man to be glorified! For no other creature can sing praise to the gods. Hence mankind has gods whose goal is to see humanity praise them, raise their pride and glorify them (the Tanach, the Bible and the Qur'an propagate this). Feed their immortality it is. This way men can take control of the gods and even destroy them.

An eyebrow raiser for you now: the movement from poly-theism (the pantheons) that Judaism, Christianity and Islam are proud of was *in fact* born of clashes of the gods (communities claiming being for god this but not that), eventually one com-munity moving out with its god declaring theirs the supreme one. Isn't that what Abraham did? Yes Abraham's was a move to find a place he would exercise his chosen god - one he regarded supreme above all others. But in essence all the gods have their origin in the MOON. Archaeologists know well why the moon represented the first, most adorable god from time immemor-ial. The moon stood out as the most certain change-maker above all other things prehistoric hunter-gatherers knew. The moon brought changes, possibilities and natural provisions. It thus signified the earliest concept of a *vanguisher,* a god. It is *paganus.* To the chagrin of 'unitarianists' – religions that believe God is one – their ideas and instructions of one god hail from a pantheon, off which an eventually 'revered son' *Nanna* was born. But the god Nanna had two sexually fertile parents. He had brothers and sisters, he had a wife, he had sons and daugh-ters and he was the firstborn. You once wondered why most so-cieties and religions strongly held the *firstborn* with higher re-gard? Now you know. Ancient religions considered the firstborn a manifestation of god.

The ancient Greeks at least maintained the relativeness of the gods in their pantheon. The place of Nanna is being occu-pied by the firstborn son of the Titans – Zeus.

The ancient Greek narrative is informative of some facts despite itself being mythological. One, that powers however strong they are do end. Two, that weak generations are respon-sible for the end of eras. But how? How on earth do the weak-lings come to take advantage of the strong? Well, the weak generations take advantage of their inherited 'parts of strength' to create formidable attackers (the Krakens/the mortal sons of gods – as read above) that in the end destroy the status quo. Third, that all this has roots (as per many narratives recycled over the ages) in the destruction of the old norms, morals and traditions and beliefs. Through challenging the knowledge created and left by previous generations new eras replace the aging ones... This is the truth about civilizations.

Ur is in utter ruins rarely remembered... Babylonia is but a memory so distant. Ancient Egypt has mummies and pyramids to tell the story of life gone...

Modern Civilization Following Old Paths

Today, many people wonder why profanities are rapidly rising and that movements and ideas against traditions – including existence of God – are growing by the day. They wonder that atheism (an intellectual creation per se) is becoming today's crown prince. Atheism is growing in the movies. Atheism is ruling in politics. It is rooting firmly in preschools, in colleges, in the sciences and in the arts generally. Many do not know this isn't new in the history of civilizations. There happens to be a cycle of these things. All ancient hegemons did witness this typical renewal and awakening. And such awakening only arise when an order is at its peak and starting to crash down.

Profanities are the last missiles hedonists hurl on God. For example, the bible (Genesis 19) says of a once vicious homosexuality that at its height took people hostage and dictated their lives – it would later be named Sodomy. People of Sodom and Gomorrah would shut neighbourhoods and declare exhaustive sex orgies. The orgies involved compulsory screwing each other in a throbbing chain of asshole fucks. Call a spade a spade. Newcomers were regarded fresh assholes to be screwed without delay. There was at the peak no quarter given, you see? One had to be in (read how Lot is being hard-pressed to comply, he was a stranger in the land of the plains). If you reread that story over and over, you learn this lesson: that since those days the practice of homosexuality is commanded, not left private to those willing. It tends to be forced up on the society including those who don't see its worth. Hence the US's September 20, 2011 suspension of the Don't Ask, Don't Tell (DADT) policy perfectly follows the path. The policy was overturned (in effect) because it wasn't enough to have gays (sodomy, considered a profanity by many) not publicised. They want it not only freely but popularly presented. They would rather have it vocal to attract many more to sodomy. Make it colourful – as colourful as the rainbow – than straight guys make their sexual relationship. That is, homosexuality at an edge above heterosexuality.

The path to moral depravity must go alongside refusal of the ideas of 'a god' in whom moral directives emanate. Why it is necessary to refute existence of a god before a people can destroy themselves? Because retaining God/gods inhibits the freedoms that embrace immorality. To embrace full immorality, a people need first of all, to have no shackles from traditional values, beliefs. In the story of Sodomy (considered true in Judaism, Christianity and Islam) we learn what a comfort/pleasure ridden society *usually* diverts into. Tasting and using the differences. It dares revoke the fundamental values of society. For example, an anus is becoming an equal of (sometimes more expensive than) a vagina. Well, soon some animal phalluses will be an equal (or better than) a man's penis. There we have the dawn of bestiality.

After all, for a serious lawyer who knows his stuff, there is bigger possibility to win a case for bestiality in the US high Courts than was for homosexuality. The same clauses of the Constitution that won Lawrence v. Texas can cleanly be gleaned to win a lawsuit for bestiality. That is, people who want to fuck their animals stand better chance to make sense in a competent Court of high instance. But that successful hunt for pleasures will continuously spew: immorality, arrogance, shamelessness and gross irresponsibility. All these being the results of unencumbered emotions and limitless freedoms. Freedoms. Yeah!

Today, for instance, there are hundreds of thousands fucking sex dollies a night. That is freedom. A liberal element to free oneself from human interrelationship. This is for you people out there who want to know how smart this learned world is doing...

I am trying to show that hegemons 'muster' empires through limitless thinking, learning, adapting, deriding, ambitious exploiting and uninhibited scheming. No barricades are left unattended. Personal pleasures rank higher on the rungs of the ladder of personal wiles – remember Woodrow's philosophy on new freedoms and individualism? It is central to the current philosophy of neoliberalism.

Via ill-wills per se leading nations limit the moral growth and sustenance of 'other people', taking advantage or physically crippling what 'nations-other' believe in. Amongst others, leading economies impose immorality on their victims through some claims of 'enlightening' or 'helping to know well'. This is a class in history. And this is the heck; on growing larger for themselves, superpowers grapple with stability of thought. Their conscience become chaotic - as in the mathematics theory of '*chaos*'. The path is not clear although every things they do are connected. As powerful and complex polities, they can disguise the shams they play and tend to argue they are playing the best *humanely* possible (the US's political elites make this claim innumerably). And it is at this time they invest heavily in knowledge and teach fields they want people to justify. Currently, for example, do you know how many millions of dollars the US corporates, States and federal government are investing in professors, PhDs, Masters and undergrads doing studies in gender issues? How much in homosexuality? How much in feminism? How much in the sociology of sex? Actually, how much in all those fields whose research results are meant to contravene (whack the stability of thought) the social traditions of the US and the world at large? This investment is done at a global scale. Universities world over are receiving bursaries from USA and the West to beseech those fields. Unsuspecting boys and girls from a hundred plus countries on earth are crisscrossing the world, going for training or development in those fields. Their ultimate impact is to come home to assault their countries' pre-existing social setup and beliefs. They are coming home to 'bedevil' their societies. So clever the US is riding.

If one applies for a postgrad scholarship (a two years master's degree, say) to train in biophysics and another applies for a PhD in gender studies (say: on ways to sustain women leadership in a third world economy), surely the gender brain is going to be half way in his studies before the biophysicist can receive promising responses. Evidences for this are for the asking amongst third world scholars. Why? Because when the US says this or that is good for human, it becomes a money mine.

So goes it in religions, culture, politics and human rights...

Isn't that what America does? Yes. She did and she still does. America thinks she is very bright, Mrs Right. That she chooses for the world to follow. But she has never been righteous. America's noble, neoliberal democracy for example rose replaying the manuals of the ancient Roman republic. A very barbaric democracy in its ways. Rome was a warlike, slavery democracy. America, foremost, took other humans into raging slavery and crashing servitude (for centuries). America's economy grew on the shoulders of boiling black slaves plus robbed lands of annihilated natives. America, like Old Rome, therefore set off while devaluing the human worthiness. That is neglecting the unity of humanity and thus making slaves (other people) nothing but properties – to trade, to kill, to geld and to rape as easy as their holders found erections to help it. The Native Americans were for centuries hunted down like hogs, penned in inglorious spots and killed wantonly through gassing and/or poisoning. There you have the background to America's democracy that is *now* the champion of human rights...

Humanity Is Elusive

One wonders how far resilient humanity is. Whatever traps are put in place humanity disentangles. For empires – however savvy they grow and pretentious they shape up – do end. Ending is a must. No empire ever survived all times but humanity is here for you to see. This says a lot. Amongst them that men remain after empires are in ashes. Men continue to struggle on this little planet after their religions are dead and forgotten. Men continue to need each other thousands of years after their self-righteous, bully states are bygones. Would you believe today the Greeks are looking to Germany, hands extended, to bail them out of an economic meltdown?

The study of how stubborn mankind is, is in itself a marvel.

Where, for example, is the old democratic pantheon of Rome? The scourge is gone. No one alive knows where the foundations of Pella – the Macedonian seat of Alexander the Great – had been built. Pella went to ruins, then to rabbles. After that she kissed the sands and left human memories. Not even the oldest of families in the North of Greece today know where Alexander lived. Pella, the bastion of 'boy lovers' (an early, public Greek homosexuality) went into oblivion and is hanging there. If the general-cum-warlord Gaius Julius Caesar could rise, see what Rome is and compare her to 'world-others' he certainly would cry. For to him non-Romans seemed no more than Rome's pukes, or, at their best, shadows of Rome. He would wonder *his* Italy degenerated into *small* men none like his contemporaries. Outdone by the 'realities of time' Italians today are the underdogs of the industrial West. One hears they cannot even keep stable their economy. Majority classy Westerners today are people Caesar left mere brutes. And poachers of monkeys...

Rome and Pella were great when majority of lands in the world were but colonised by clubs of monkeys or still had races walking naked. Said bluntly; many lands had people without knowledge nudity has a disgusting sight. For many still mistook nudity for natural clothes – as a fact they couldn't change.

The examples above show how accursed greatness is. After some knowledge have entered them, 'the greats' think they are the measure of the goods that can ever be. I show herein that the USA thinks she is the best that mankind has ever been. For example, she deems herself the 'trailblazer' of best ideas. It is Washington that is headquarter of idealism. Yet that illusion has over histories been the worst mistake civilizations do. By asserting for herself 'best of heads' status, American elites elect themselves 'best of humanity'. And thus task their minds with a mission to bring the rest to light – the American burden. Count in factors brought in by the economy and modern technologies there you have the simplified causes of neo-colonialism – eventually the reasons globalism is raging.

Simply defined: neo-colonialism is a calculated chauvinistic expansion to other lands in ways less palpable. Today the USA is the de facto neo-colonialist. She is colonising ideas, motivations, technologies, economies and the dreams of other nations. The American Dream for example is mother of other nations' dreams. The White House sneezes, the world catches cold. This, my reader, was the very import of Woodrow Wilson's school of idealism. His view centred on exporting the needs of the USA to attempt solving his country's ulterior 'motives' using foreign countries' potentials. You wonder all other nations are obsessed with democratic globalism. Yet, in a nutshell, 'Woodrow wanted the world for the USA'. And Woodrow won his way, wouldn't you say? But then, idealism is based on ideas and ideas are infinite...

It has turned out to be a no one's ground.

America In The Footprints Of Ancient Rome

Gone are civilizations this planet ever held. Yet Rome is the most remembered *maybe* because she was the latest of the real great ancients. Or because she had well established record keeping – they kept detailed annals of events and a register of the deeds of great men. Could it be because she ran longer than any other empire before and after her? Is it because her traditions spilled all over the 'old world' such that they would later be exported widely? Exported through: migrations, settlements and colonization? Whatever the reason(s) is/were, Rome is well documented.

In old Rome – during the republican era – a select few occupying the Senate ruled. They were headed by one(s) of their own

– the 'Consul'. Oftentimes there were two 'consuls' at a go. Flip back the times and you have the USA run by the same arrangement. There is the Senate and Congress altogether replaying the Roman Senate. And just like Rome, the two are based at the *Capitol* Hill. In America, the Consul is replayed by a President. Power in Rome was secured through senatorial and gubernatorial political intrigues. That is your USA as well. Apart from that it took winning of pervasive wars of invasions done by the legions. The wars created honours to the generals. Wars brought gold, food (mainly supply of staples/grains) and respect to Rome. The legions were thus the true creators of Rome's wealth and her blunt diplomacies.

Who creates wealth and diplomacy for the USA? The US Army does... just like the legions. The military might scaffolds the US diplomacy and hence acts as the stabilizer (?or inverter) of her mega economy... Read on, you have got a treat.

...in the Last Days of America's Hegemony (13)

Without the Armies' extra usefulness beyond defence, would America be this rich? If yes, how so? This sounds simple a question for those who take things lightly. But an answer to it would run a full discourse. I give a no for an answer.

America isn't rich, feared and loved in equal measures because she has best humans. Neither because she has better knowledge of life nor the most rational judgments on issues. But because of what her military can/do.

The status of her military is of an investment – a huge one surpassing almost all others. It generates wealth directly and indirectly. For example, by America becoming a bud of Kuwait other nations shy from attacking (or making any unfair dealings with) the latter. The nations fear how the US Army would answer to that. From this, only this 'Metternichian' setup, the US generates billions of dollars from Kuwait's oil reserves. This is clever, uh! The US has this replayed over and over amongst almost all Allies. One should give credits where they are due. The Pentagon is clever. It knows how to make hard cash.

Did the ancient kingdoms of Europe: the Gallic, Germanic, Briton, Spanish, Greek and other polities fear and love Rome because she had the best human rules? For the reason that she had a republican system with a rich, arguing, democratic Senate? Or for the pompous belief by Romans that they were best humans? No. No. No. The Roman republic had an outstanding, most disciplined, well-trained and brutal military machinery. It was known as the 'legions'. When the legions fought on foreign lands they killed with abandon. Rivers of Europe filled human blood. Fear struck the spines of all who lived to tell the legions' carnage. And respect of Rome ensued from cowed survivors. Terrorism carried the days. And it always won...

There were times the Roman Republic turned Europe into a field of war. The Roman swords known as '*gladii*' were once the most widespread weapon outnumbering all Romans. Each silver, gold or bronze coin that went to Rome was raised either by wars, manufacturing of *gladii* or looting foreign lands. Wars brought boots, political negotiations, business alliances, tithes, slaves and of course colonial occupations. Wars were diplomatic. Wars fastened Rome's Patriotism.

The Romans were so patriotic when killing. Widespread killings of their perceived enemies were meant to send message to distant defenders that Rome was great. The legionnaires sang 'blood for Rome, honour to Rome'. Make no mistake about this, it is a tradition still living today.

Troops of occupation such as US soldiers in Haditha (Iraq) sang and boasted of patriotism as they killed little girls, old moms and poor daddies. Respect for America – so they were heard shouting in the middle of the night. And all this as cold murders continued. With all that they argued they were defending America. One wonders whether the word 'defence' isn't a philosophical specie amongst Americans...

The idea of military bases? Yeah. When she lasted the Roman republic not only had legions stationed far off – looking at the noses of their victims – but also had war machineries, military chests and legionnaires crawling all over (spying over the) foreign territories. Legionnaires' camps were magnificent forts built on top of hills across all strategic places Rome's shadow reached. America isn't a pioneer of camping around the world – erecting strategic military bases – to 'defend imperial interests'. That is an old, colonial trick. Rome exhausted this trick to the core.

For all I know, it is a tradition predating Rome and Macedonia – read more on this in part 18 and 19 herein.

Rome Is Gone

Scholars do agree Rome was so much of a strong empire. A

power whose innovations in war techniques, military occupations, the navies, taxations, democracy, debates in Senate, patriotic rants and chants and heroism were unequalled.

Often unnoticed by many who read the history of ancient Rome is that all those *innovations* depended on some socially ingrained philosophical stances to sustain them. Nobilities philosophised, politicians idealised and then the poor paid the price. This balance was well unbalanced - you can easily see this by yourself. It shows that the poor (the commoners) took the blunt.

The problem of 'philosophy' is that it nourishes the mind much than it cares for the body. It bears men with strong mind, yes, but weak bodies. This is a fact you should note: weak bodies *waste* the state. For example, Rome's power philosophies (mainly were of sophistry strands and the machtpolitik) encouraged too much investment in the mind to manipulate the people. The Romans. This weakened the toiling bodies of common Romans. The weakened bodies would later become the driving cause for her demise. Say, the setting was the last straw that broke the camel's back. For it, at last, created ease minds inside weakened bodies (minds that sought pleasures and pride than anything else).

In America today, the weakened bodies (of the common citizens) that are growing so pompous of pleasures and pride are driven by some philosophies of liberalism...

Reflect now on Rome: she had grown from the strength of the mind (philosophical strength), and she went down because of the same. That says, 'what goes around comes around'.

Rome's Pallbearers

Rome ran the longest course than any other empire before her did and would do afterwards. Her demise was so gradual that scholars until today fail to pinpoint at what exact time she eased downhill.

Some choose to say her very rising sowed the seeds of decline.

An argument meaning she started declining the moment she rose (that is, she was built on a wrong set of ideas).

Others argue that at the start of excessive bickering amongst the senators, beginning within the last century of the republic (after 100BC) which led to several civil wars, was the start of her demise. They argue that at this point the 'cult of personality' politics became predominant and thus killed the honour of the Roman citizenship.

Brighter still are those who argue that by the time Rome's leading houses – the *patres*/patricians – degenerated into a preening lot, instead of remaining pragmatists, demise was inevitable. There are many other less comprehensive views.

Rome's decline is shrouded in mysteries scholars do not appreciate specific reasons.

I tend to look at Rome's decline as resulting from increased socio-political 'knowledge'. I hold this view for the USA as well.

Throughout my investigations of relationship between people and power, I find that scholars overlook the effects of increased knowledge amongst the people whose empire has to metamorphose (I mean citizens at the core of a polity). Scholars do not think 'the people' beyond being 'instruments of imperial productivity'. - that is the human agency for empire control. I put forward that in practice knowledge accumulation alters the citizens. But rarely do the rulers acknowledge this.

The rulers of empires have over the ages immersed in politics of material relationship and bullying other nations mainly. And thus the rulers have been exercising power without getting alarmed their people's conscience is shifting. Slowly but surely, the people mature to resent (now openly) what their states stand for. They form new interpretations of who they are. These are interpretations that, frequently, part ways with the status quo. For example, in the last days of Rome the Romans gradually got wary of the Senate and the rationale of its powers. The Romans then grew uninterested in what the men at the capitol stood for. They steadily caught up with realisation of the games of numbers used to dupe them (as I discussed previously about the US democracy) and the games' destructive spirit.

In the USA today, a chunk of the population is already watching her chauvinistic policies with disdain. One can now easily discern most Americans are wary of the Capitol. The Senate and the Congress are now viewed, by the educated mass mainly, as some clever fellows who reap where they didn't sow. Recently, citizens are standing against a host of policies the law makers seem interested with. Evident is that the people are parting ways with Washington's traditional power politics. For example, Americans are becoming sharply anti-war. And the erstwhile cherished American heroism is losing its appeal. Boys and girls joining the US Army today are taking it as a job, not as a call of patriotism.

When she lasted Rome had a core of people looking at her achievements, richness, lifestyle and social fabric to refute they could ever stoop. They saw 'world-others' as hordes of animals, irrational barbarians, damn villains, mere lunatics! They idolised Rome 'the navel' of civilizations and head of global pantheons. That Rome was the homeland of gods – they said. Being the home of all gods assured the citizens Rome would remain forever.

We know better – Rome is gone. Master time mastered her time. She succumbed to her own games. And her sons were her pallbearers...

Is The Us Faring Better?

We know she is not. The US as a hegemon is built on foundations worse than Rome was. For example, like Rome the US retains the same killer innovations discussed above - although in the case of USA they are at a note higher. America has unprecedented massive money guzzling military bases, costlier war technologies, diplomacy based on bogus alliances or enmities etc. More than those the USA delights in 'heroism and patriotism' that in the end cultivate economic drudgery for a majority. Yet America isn't in the times Rome were. Her people are faster learners. Modern, global states are cleverer with people more united, very sophisticated and sharp to adapt. The age of borderless digital information sharing has brought quick reciprocation to whatever goes around. These weren't realities of the day when Rome partied on her subjects. Greeks were again so divided a century following the failure of Hellenization movement. Gaul was tens of polities that vied amongst themselves.

Above all those, Rome's spirit of acquisitiveness however nasty it was, couldn't become half as foolish as America's. America's love of wealth is unequalled this far... And her political elites want to hear none of their being dead minded wealth making lot...

Things remain the same more they change.

Looking at their achievements, Americans in the Senate and Congress think they are the best politicos there ever have been. Best of brains they think they are. So, they stand hallowed in beautiful tailor-made tuxedos and think they are righteous to set standards for the whole world. All those they do (they decide and give directives) although they have no clue how a desert *sheikh* struggles to get bread on the family table. Or how an African leader, an ex-rebel, views this treacherous world.

Again, just like old Rome, America's lawmakers are self-aggrandising proclaiming a single global law. And a single moral ground for countries. That is, one view of the world and how the politics of other countries should behave! Behave 'they' as born in Washington. Behave as viewed from Washington by politicians whose pay-cheques are the fattest in the world.

Those Roman '*Washingtoners*' are ignorant of the least struggles a third world farmer ventures through to reap her sweat. History has had this kind of arrogance ...

SECTION FIVE: READING THE PAST

...in the Last Days of
America's Hegemony (14)

In this part let me point out a list of selected, well documented and most observable realities known to dominate society during the days of decline of the Roman polity, republic and eventually the empire.

Meanwhile, place in your mind a mirror image that reflects the salient realities of society as far as the US is concerned.

Be quick to detect patterns and parallels. Within each point I make here don't miss to see deep in America's: society, military, culture, wealth, knowledge and politicos' dispositions. This is because they are all in there.

When I drive home these parts (that this section calls 'Reading the Past') you will have learned that the factors I discuss here are not applicable to the US and Rome strictly. They make the dusky hours of almost all empires. Then the last two concluding parts (part 20 and 21) tell in details why these facts are universal and have remained so over the Ages.

Before Rome Eased Downhill...

...in the last days of Rome, politicians (in the Senate - Patricians and the representatives of the people) became frequently entrenched in personal triumphs and self-assertion. The two kept steadily growing, eventually they bred backroom alliances, sectarianisms and divisions somehow concealed from the public eyes yet vigorously vying. This made Senate sittings occasions for meeting of clashing egos, partisanships (Populares versus Optimates) and the Senators mainly employed personal attacks to win argument against each other (*argumentum ad hominem*). Another was an excessive prevalence of 'attack of reason'. The Senators thus avoided republican politics in favour of personal vanities. This would eventually culminate into a 'cult of personality' politics. A democracy wherein Generals Pompey and Caesar personify the late Roman republic.

...in the last days of Rome, self-interests amongst the leading, private citizens (the Patricians, mostly) overtook the concerns for the fate of the republic. Consequent to this 'favours' (based on partisanships and/or bloodlines) were guided by the need to support the inner-circles of friends for consulship, army generalship, legateship, 'tribuneship' and the governorship of conquered territories. When Augustus Octavian held power for example, even marrying was controlled/interfered with for political expediency. He would tell a senator, a friend or an aide to divorce who and marry who – when and how. Mark Anthony is one of many who suffered that practice. This practice helped the patricians earn kickbacks. It created an environment of bondage and provided personal vanities to the Senators and the clients who fell in the cycle – of course subject to practical circumstances.

...in the last days of Rome, the political structure of the republic got enveloped in a system of ubiquitous hand-outs. The system got so complex *over times* with hundreds then thousands of patrons and unlimited clients. It was a matrix surrounding almost each influential Senator. It was known as *clientela*. It was a *scheme* that kept in place an algorithm of voting in the Senate and passage of convenient herd based rules e.g. war making decisions and laws. The patrons and their clients made a strong column that smoothened money changing hands far and wide. Hence they made a legalised conduit of corruption. It was an early prototype of today's lobbying schemes.

...in the last days of Rome, the military complex (the Roman legions: I tend to call them 'the unfortunate Roman boys') was the handiest institution top politicians owned. It consumed the lion's share of Rome's budget. Millions of *sesterces* a month. This pecuniary payload went largely in the weaponry department (it was a structural arrangement, rather). Manufactured and maintained were military grade: *gladii*, daggers, onagers, *harpax*, catapults, scorpion bows, axes and spears/javelins (*hastae*). These military grade stuffs exceeded the number of Roman citizens. Military field engineering piled more on that industry. Rome was an economy based on militarism and violent manoeuvres. Thus the legions (the boys) were primary investment yet outcomes of their exploits went to the fewest possible old men bickering day in day out in the Forum.

...in the last days of Rome, prosperity amongst the leading classes particularly members of the primary houses (the patricians), successful army generals, legates, tribunes etc. made them richer such that disparities in wealth became clear cut. The majority (the poor: the wretched citizens and the slaves) worked hard but their labour ended in drudgery. This was unlike the patricians who continued building huge palaces (villas) for pleasure. Those expensive houses were used as forts for home security. Big stables were built for horses' breeds. Patricians owned big swimming pools for cooling their bodies and hectares of domestic gardens for leisure. Yet the richest Rome as she then was, crawled with majority *extremely* poor who slept rough, earned through servitude, turned themselves up into slavery and took to prostitution for a living. All the activities they performed made sure they would end up living lifelong toilers.

...in the last days of Rome, the military forts (camps) and army outposts became the marks of Rome's military presence in her dominions. These included colonies and the lands of the so called 'allies'. On most geographical locations that mattered, Rome had her legions manning barbarians (subjects were barbarians as per Romans' world view), natural wealth, trade routes, tithes, Roman settlements, allies (puppets) and renegades alike. Allies and renegades were to be secured against their own people. Romans had as many imperial camps as possible and kept there many legions and staff than there were in Rome. This says: the legions guzzled a lot of wealth whilst remaining political outsiders. Only 'the noisy old men' remained the insiders.

...in the last days of Rome, new wealth flowed in mainly from outside. It came from colonies, dominions, the Roman settlements and the whining allies (puppets). These inflows made Rome the seat of global wealth. Gold and silver were money and Rome had the best valued of them such that each 'strong man' could mint his own money therefrom. With wealth notwithstanding, the ordinary citizens grew poorer and desperate while a few families of nobilities concentrated wealth, power and other influences. The result(s) of this arrangement enabled *some* nobilities to outplay both the republic, the citizens and the Roman democracy.

...in the last days of Rome, the politics of the republic degenerated into politics of individuals (see? The oldest traces of political liberalism and individualism). It included competitions amongst the figures who could muster the Senate and/or popular support. It became politics for those who could offer coins, give favours, roll out expensive parties, command legions and do better rhetoric. An amazing part of it is that in most cases these individuals (they were populists) happened to be the most ruthless and self-centred aristocrats (examples: general Marius and Sulla). They were slave owning nobilities (and thus holders of means of livelihoods) who could not envision a stubborn future beyond the usual nuisances of idealism on the glories of the present and the past.

...in the last days of Rome, imagination about the polity (the state/the republic) and the world at large that Romans had were based on two philosophies: One, 'people as power'. Two, 'might as right'. The citizens were therefore taught extreme forms of patriotism that encouraged the youth to join legions without hesitation. It was popularised as a matter of life and death. This was to make the youth prove Rome had people, people who meant power. The youth thus lived to show Rome's muscles and arrogance. As a result the youth remained a constant lot for war sacrifices. The lambs for sacrifice. To the rulers of Rome, the world was a place for 'showdowns' and competitions. Any other territory had to be with or against Rome. And 'with' meant 'submission' whilst 'against' meant being in 'violent competition'.

There was no neutrality.

...in the last days of Rome, the Romans in the city eventually grew restless and brave enough they dared challenge the city's status quo. Talk of the idealism of 'people as power' backfiring! Recorded are tumultuous occasions involving inner-city terrorism, marauding ex-servicemen killing and robbing the citizens, rampages from buildings torching gangs (the Capitol got burnt several times) and the senators earned deep hatred. As citizens of Rome killed fellow citizens through terrorism, Rome grew shaky and horrified. The legions were nowhere to help because they were away fighting foreigners. All these happened despite her efficient military powers and good propaganda mechanics...

Some things never change... And humanity is so elusive. You are going to learn this the more you read on...

Civilisations Are A Continuum

The greatness of Rome is gone – disappeared although not forgotten. From the ashes, the philosophies and material foundations of what Rome was have come stories of greatness, grandeur, achievement, valour and the signs of what human societies are capable of.

Rome was ahead of her time in some respects, scholars do admit. Her achievements were so remarkable and undeniable they are great heritage to later generations. They are well remembered. And some of them have been reworked overtime.

But wait! They are all meaningless – in the end. The famous acts of valour, heroism, bravery and the daring said of Romans were not as precious as they got fabled. Otherwise their greatness wouldn't be gone. It would remain forever as is the price of gold that for thousands of years still holds high. *Perhaps* this is because Rome didn't, realistically speaking, achieve all she is famed for... A greater part, obviously the core of what we call Roman, she inherited from some ancient societies that went before her.

Put Rome's achievements on a bisecting, deductive lens and one should see that 'life has seen a *progression* of some kind. Progressing, linearly or not, 'civilisations have been a continuum'. Rome was another recipient/an inheritor of majority thoughts the ancient societies before her had gathered. No wonder she became excellent. For all she had was to learn, adapt and improvise...

I make a stand: that the old Romans weren't exceptional at all. Rather they were faster learners. Only that they were quicker in adopting to knowledge that existed before them.

What we learn from Rome tell us that humanity has seen continuities. And *that* more than exceptionalities. Nations, Civilizations and Empires across epochs have only differed based on the quality of continuities they improvised up on/from. This is easily verifiable through phenomenological analysis of historical facts. And this knowledge should pre-empt those who *may* think they are the best part of humanity.

Well, to shine a light on that we have a brief catch-up to do.

A simplified recap: 'Rome was a granddaughter to Ancient Greece'. Say, there once was old Greece, great and mighty she would ever get. The Greeks – in Milesia, Ephesus, Korinthos, Athens, Sparta, Macedonia and in some myths like *Troy* were precursors to what would become Rome.

The Romans greatly adapted from the Old Greeks such that in some traditions Romans allude to being (revere of having been) descendants of some mythical Greek geniuses and a god(s). As one reads on the possible origin of Romans gravity pulls towards ancient Greece and mysterious god(s). Well, the 'demigods' illusion in the Roman narratives is nothing (can be overlooked for good reason) because it is but an ancient Greek world view. The old Greeks had an underlying assumption (at the core of their ideas) that to be superhuman or a creature of immense capacities (mental faculties mostly) it needed one to be 'part human, part god'. They viewed mankind as essentially in need of sharing godhead to be excellent and powerful. The Greeks were always craving for immortality. And to them immortality was only possible with recourse to the powers of the gods. That is how even their *very* heroes ended up being deified – read the story of Achilles and others.

The Romans extensively continued Greek traditions. They pursued Greek learning and lesson contents. They continued believing in a pantheon and held onto the idea of immortalisation of personal deeds through heroics. Their heroes do great things so as to be well remembered many generations after them. In short, they maintained the Greek social theory.

The Romans inherited an excessive philosophising than was practical learning and/or application of nature. That included inventing and portraying 'heroes' as primary beings necessary for fulfilment of humanity or continued innovation of imagination.

So, one learns that a host of great figures in the Old Roman history were spurred to usefulness by the Old Greek stories of daring, adventure and bravery (read: the Iliad and Odyssey amongst others). Also the myth of fighting swords' masters, 'Achilles and Hector', have had great impact throughout the Western epics and literature. Too late did the Old Romans (under semi-literate Augustus Octavian) learn practical knowledge: amongst them, civil engineering and architectural skills. The timing of that shift would rather prove it was because they had opened up to non-Greek ideas including Egyptians'.

Before Augustus his mentor and predecessor, Gaius Julius Caesar, had gone to Egypt at the head of thousands of his men. With him was the whole entourage of the Roman brain - young nobles and skilled fighters. They stayed for months. There he learned invaluable lessons about the earth, the universe, faith and others. Caesar would come back home not only awed by the Egyptian learning but also with strong resolve that Egyptians were well ahead of Rome in some respects. That even their sense of time and seasons of the year, movement of heavenly bodies such as stars, moon, the sun etc. were well ahead and made better sense. He thus adapted, with minor changes, the Egyptian calendar (making the Julian calendar) and interpretation of fate, eventually declaring himself 'god' in the tradition of Egyptian royalty. Had he lived longer, Caesar would have made an Egypt out of Rome!

Egyptian ideas on the other hand (Egypt in the 'last hours' of the first century BC) were a mixture of local, oriental and other exotic thinking that had accumulated over a long history of learning, diffusion and contact. That is *briefly* how the Middle Eastern factor first came to Rome...

Before I wind up this treatise I will have shown that the

boastful ancient Greeks were themselves (largely) copycats. Some people elsewhere had a long time before Greeks lived and passed on most ideas Greeks are pampered with. I intone that the shortcomings of the Greek 'self-concept' education which later become Romans' was preponderance of philosophising and idealising and love of militancy than performance of *'physique'*. That is, the art of living in which growth of the mind takes precedence to that of physical productivity. So they had too intelligent a mind, too weak a body. This preoccupation still goes on in the current global order coached by the US of A.

There is an alarming growth of intellect against physical fitness of the people.

My purpose here is to show that life and its major ideas have seen a continuum. With many epochs adding and altering bits based on environment, human agency and the challenges of the people's time. It shouldn't be a surprise to you that America is Rome incarnate. Because the USA is largely from Rome.

Avoid getting deceived by the obvious...

From Old Rome To Washington

Whatever disputes there may arise on the nature, direction and paths of Rome's socio–economic evolution – or, whether her achievements would later become meaningless or not – at least no scholar refutes that Rome would at last dissolve *than* disappear. No one knows a timeline for Rome's downfall.

Great Rome in reality scattered all over the old world through 'bloodlines' and idealism, 'spreading' to present day Europe, parts of Asia and somewhere in North Africa. Rome fought with fortitude for her eminence – yet unbeknownst to herself she was slowly weakening – until of course her military and arrogance became fully inconsequential. In a nutshell, Rome's edifice dissolved against the factors of time.

The fall of Rome was a great dispersal that involved *extremely* subtle movements. The Romans didn't record either the beginning or progress of her decline. This because the two weren't overtly palpable. Old Rome was not fought and defeated. She got herself immersed in the ideas, steadiness and social ways of the very people she had conquered. She had come to realise the people she had believed were barbarians, uncultured, un-civilised and brutes in fact had *some* edges in many respects. One of them a comprehensive religion deemed better than the pantheon Romans believed in. For example, she slowly fell to Christianity – a pacifist Jewish sect. How beautiful this is! It is a story of a pacifist's messages (Christ's teachings) which went to conquer the militants (Old Romans).

The Roman governors of Jerusalem all their times there be-lieved Jews were one dirty, distasting, insensitive, preposterous and violent 'race' that had nothing of worth but senselessness and noise. Time would prove the Romans wrong as they soon fell to the teachings and messages of a Jewish mystic - Jesus of Nazareth.

Years later especially after the Middle Ages, even the Roman tongue – Latin – scattered. The tongue almost got washed away before its debris froze into French, Portuguese, Italian and Spanish. These languages are essentially Latin. Other Romans got completely swallowed by languages distant from Latin amongst them the Celtic, Angles, Saxon and other Germanic speeches.

But centuries later the scattered 'Rome' would regroup and show up. This time Old Rome was tailored in a patched coat with resplendent colours. The birth of America. Rebirth of Rome.

The Great Gathering

Briefly stated: hunger, dreams, ambitions, arrogance, hope and some embers of adventurism would later regroup the Romans. They singularly and independently from each other crossed the Atlantic to America (between the 15th and the 20th centuries) where they resettled 'violently' as *carpetbaggers* colo-nialists. They shipped in big numbers over the centuries. There they found America. They found the USA. Another Rome born far off...

Americans Belong To The God Yahweh

It might get millions of Americans ashamed to learn that they are a nation of God. As atheism keeps looming, one's association with God seems illogical in front of magnificent sciences. Yet one must remind Americans that they rose in the grace of a god – YAHWEH of the Jewish traditions. This is a fact.

Take or leave it. So it will remain forever.

Having been almost entirely colonised and/or influenced by the old imperial Rome (it was firmly under Christianity from the 4th century Anno Domino) the Christian Rome converted Europe to Christ. Christ subsists in he who sent him – a supposed god of (the patriarchies) Abraham, Isaac and Jacob. The three followed a god now famous as Jehovah. It was thus a conversion to a god known as YAHWEH. A god whose son is called Jesus Christ and whose works reside in a holy ghost. Thus 'in the name of the father, the son and the holy ghost, Amen' Americans grew praying.

At the core of the mind of the founders of America was therefore the Christian social philosophy. That is, the Christian interpretation of life, death, human relationship, christian family upbringing and the fate of societies. The USA wholesomely acceded to that and thus nationally 'In God We Trust' they declared.

If one could turn back the time and visualise what went on in the five centuries of earnest migrations, one would see the Atlantic Ocean a ghosts filled Sea. Thousands of ships ventured the Atlantic from Europe to mainland America but less made it. Hundreds of vessels capsized each year killing hundreds or thousands of hopeful emigrants. Hundreds of ships *listed* killing hundreds or thousands of people on-board through hunger, starvation and diseases. Hurricanes, gales, fronts, maelstroms and all manners of see monsters feasted on hundreds or thousands of the 'would-be' Americans, laying good men to waste. The dead became ghosts – some would swear!

This bad news went back home in Europe or reached relatives who had made it to America. Scared and sorrowful, the hardened seafarers moved on. But all they had was 'a prayer'.

Navigation was at the lowest of its possible technologies in the last five centuries. And weather studies were almost guesswork – nothing in it sure to call a science. Death and luck were the most certain. But emigrants had no choice, they needed out.

Given the menace to life there were, the brave would-be Americans fully turned to God. On boarding their ships in Europe all they had was hope in God. They hoped that they would safely make it through. Prayers rang from evenings to mornings and lasted the daytimes. The prayers were mainly that 'oh God, in you we Trust' and 'our lives are yours God'. All the days they made and called penance. No man remains brave when facing certain death. With that penance they safely crossed to America.

If it were re-created in the 3D movies, one would listen to some big roars of prayers. Murmurs and shouts from combined hundreds of thousands of ships carrying migrants across the Atlantic. All prayers in the name of God.

The Jewish god YAHWEH.

And when they reached America and were perfectly footed, Americans remembered their deliverer. They used an old word to refer to him say 'providence'. With exacting reverence, the American settlers enshrined this submission saying their mission had been allowed by providence i.e. *Annuit Coeptis*.

Fast forward to the 21st century; *many* Americans have forgotten who got them where they are. It is like the Old Jews forgetting he who had delivered them from captivity and led them mysteriously across the 'Sea of Reeds'. As usual, the old Roman arrogance has come home to roost. Like the old Jews, Americans now need a golden 'calf' to while their time with.

Well, a golden calf will soon be born. Its mother is atheism. Today like in the old. 'Birds of a feather flock together'.

Rome – Reconfigured

The current USA is, like Old Rome, a 'hegemony' built on the spirit of 'acquisitiveness'. And wishful dreams of grandeur. The American dream, so they call it. But the American Dream is a material dream. A dream of acquiring as much as one can. In other words, 'wealth is life' is the dream. This says why America like her ancestor – Rome – is increasingly undergoing moral depravity and an alarming poverty of virtues. All these despite her material achievement becoming excessive. The leading 'elements' in the USA are partly Latin or have at one time in ancestry been subjects of Rome. Or under the shadows of great Rome they lived. So there is that Roman cunning in them...

I fore-stated in this part that Rome was a philosophically couched imperial power. At this point one has to acknowledge what all those 'American colonialists' had in common from a shared Roman background and/or ancestry: idealism. They either had survived Rome's arm-twisting or had been her sphere of influence at one time. So they had/have that Roman Idealism at heart. No wonder therefore they are INHERITORS of Roman arrogance and philosophies of power. No wonder the US is as muscular and warlike as was old Rome. It's from a father to a son.

Scattered many they had become, regrouped one they became i.e. from many we are one. One out of many (read: *E Pluribus Unum*). This is declared on the Great Seal of the United States of America.

Although the words E Pluribus Unum are embossed on the US Great Seal, they are Latin (Roman). And there is yet more there: *Novus Ordos Seclorum* which means 'New Order of the Ages'. Some choose to vary it saying the 'New World Order'. That is Roman again. Perhaps pushing further the connection might not seem a sincere academic practice. But I give it a go here.

Look, the Romans viewed themselves best of human races and the only ones capable of influencing courses of human life (idealism, again). They created an order – called the *Pax Romana* – that they regarded a paragon of peace and tranquility – intelligence and skills altogether. It included rules and morals they thought were the best ever and for which all human races were destined. We know now. That order crumbled and is in ashes. To America's founding fathers, a new order reflecting Rome's seems to have been the idea (Roman idealism, resurrected) hence 'Novus Ordos Seclorum' – new order of the Ages. It is an order based on some rules, morals and perceived thought of excellence. In the footsteps of old Rome. They blessed that intention with '*Annuit Coeptis*' which invokes the claim 'Providence approves our undertaking'.

Beautiful idealism, uh!

There certainly is too much Rome in the USA.

Inquisitive non-historians (who have ever thought it) may wonder why America is a mirror image of Rome in many ways. They fail to connect the dots, that Rome left many ideas than technical manuals (the absence of *physique* I said above). Romans were masters in idealism. Ideas they almost always ended enforcing through their harsh legions. And those ideas still live today. America is the archetype of those who gobbled Rome's ideas. If you read America's mix of political thoughts, for example, you see that her worries, materialism and ambitions are seen the Roman ways. The ways include prideful militarism, bloodletting via endless wars, a phantom democracy, projected premiership-claim and the worship of 'acquisitiveness' than any other thing...

It is the same claim of premiership that has seen the US singularly decide to trash agreements with Iran. Agreements and deals reached through rational daytimes negotiations. A deal assented to not only by the Washington and Tehran but mother Europe as well. That is an unexplained level of arrogance. Yet one well known by experts in Classical Rome. Rome never kept agreements. Rome made truces for expediency. She never had friends either... One time a polity could be Rome's friend only to become an archenemy in a blink of an eye.

The Repeat: Mistakes Of Rome, Greece

The US democracy is becoming stunningly elusive. The same way went democracy in the dusky hours of ancient Greece and Rome. Her heydays for example are *imperceptibly* getting people divorced from actual decision making (I fully treat this in some early parts of this treatise). Many a time they're caught unaware by very crucial resolutions and laws much as outsiders are. The US economy wholesomely now depends on achieved 'scales of foreign ambitions'. These are scales conceived by a few kingpins in material acquisition and disposal (Plato's drones, reread) – not the representatives of the people. This way eventually America has perfectly clad the shoes of the waning old Rome.

There is in US today – like was it in Rome two millennia ago – an ever growing overdependence on outmuscling the outsiders to ensconce America's greatness.

One of many facts known about Rome is that 'by the time she rooted her economy in her dominions, Rome became prone to outside winds'. From this context her 'societal integrity' deteriorated. Her great, foreign sourced wealth poured into a dying civilization at the Capitol. Outside, Rome had become the most coveted and hated powerhouse such that her nobilities (the Optimates and the Populares) became targets of assassinations and terrorism.

Although dying she was, yet Rome remained coveted. Coveted and hated. And the idiosyncrasies of Rome's politicians clashed, roiling the republic into petty partisanships and ego. Is the US not here yet?

Chalk down your answer...

Covet And Hate At A Go

The US is globally hated. Just like Rome was in her halcyon days, America today is. There is no question about that.

President Barack Obama's early speeches and visits outside the US, for example, were filled with words and   feigned passionate recognition of the fact that the USA had sadly made herself hated. More often he 'pretended' to decry the causes.

If one reads/listens to the President's earliest speeches one learns the US had made mistakes of taking the world for granted. She had forgotten to bother with mutual respect. And when bombing outsiders, the Pentagon had forgotten there were innocent people down there. In different parts of the world, the US military drones had been killing tens each day. As a result, America ended being coveted for what she has – her greatness, her wealth, the dollar economy – but got hated for what she is – arrogant and brutal.

With unmanned drones making tens of orphans every week, the USA smelled cadavers...

Covet and hate. One could study this if she played this experiment: Go to the most volatile part of the Arab world where the youth allege the US is evil. Give an offer to some of the youth to migrate to US. A full funded and legal migration. The result, most likely is, many will take the offer. Well, they say America is a great place to be. That is, 'covet and hate'.

President Obama explicitly admitted that *bellicose* US policies and her imperial practice were to blame. That they were causes for the 'covet and hate' global air that existed then. Take the speech he gave at the University of Cairo in 2009 – a speech named 'A New Beginning' – you learn a myriad White House admissions and frustrations to that end.

The President had ascended at a time the US relationship with the world was at an all-time low. He made promises to rectify 'overlooking' committed by previous regimes and to reinvent US attitudes towards other nations. Obama's promises went awry as he would guarantee wars in the Arab world – in Libya, Yemen and Syria for example. He also continued unencumbered supporting the *imperial* Jewish terrorism over poor Palestinians. He shored up military bases elsewhere. These to the fulfilment of Al – Qaeda's press releases following Arab fanfare at Obama's Cairo promises. And all that to *shame* the Nobel Prize Committee that had run emotional to award Obama a Peace Prize he hadn't worked for yet. Osama bin Laden and Al – Qaeda's warning were vindicated too soon. The Nobel Committee's judgment got proven wrong.

Worse still, it was at this very time European leaders (America's own allies) got informed (in an Edward Snowden spy leak) that they were under surveillance of the NSA (the National Security Agency) via telecommunications and software technologies and others. The leaks were swiftly confirmed right. That, only as a drop in a bucket full of what was going on in that direction. That immediately became a global scandal. European allies turned 'cry-babies' telling the US that isn't what she should be doing to her 'trusted friends'. Germany's Angela Merkel was solemnly devastated. She ran heaven and earth throwing words, laying blame. Well, I have stated it clearly here that the US economy isn't in for friendship or good 'neighbourhood'. It is in for business. Business by any means possible. The US economy is entirely Machiavellian.

There were many other frustrations of that likes. All of them proofs the US cannot keep her words. Not agreements. Not friendships. Because she has too much Rome in her. Her cunning precede her virtues.

Hatred had been around decades before George W. Bush and Bill Clintons. Those Presidents had continued policies considered 'bones of contention'.

I have so far shown that the US became a problem (an arrogant hegemon, a manipulator) when President Woodrow Wilson engineered the 'stateside' towards his 'idealist' perspective of international relations. That perspective transformed the US into a 'selfish' socio-economic power. With that, periods of barbaric actions ensued. There were times public political 'influencers' had to interfere with the executive's business to bring a semblance of logic and calculation. Those were times the Armies' zeal (the Pentagon's calculus of strategies) for bloodbath went nauseating, then horrifying and at most overtly disgraceful. For example, in 1973 the US Congress had to move in to veto President Richard Nixon's ceaseless shoring up of soldiers and equipment to Vietnam. Vietnam had become a war of madness and brutality – a war without honour, without end. The Congress' move led to the 'War Powers Act (1973)'. In effect the Congress Act restricted and curtailed military expenditure hence taking a stand against the infamous Vietnam War. This Act still holds today. The Act stands a warning of how far the White House can go with senselessness. It is a proof that the US executive and the Pentagon military brasses, however informed Americans think they are, can act incredulous and irrational they need strong oversight.

I entice more...

If you go back in time to 1953 you've got the saddest story of 'Operation Ajax'. This was an imperial operation in which the CIA (acting as a body of hired mercenaries) headed Britain's M16 to arm-twist and outmuscle Prime Minister Mohammad Mosaddegh of Iran. The CIA command in the operation featured Dwight D. Eisenhower, Allen Dulles and Kermit Roosevelt Jr. This was the first operation in which a US Intel Agency learned it could as well lead other nations' Intelligence units. While this earned hatred from Iranians, the gulf region and the Arab world at large, it taught lessons to the US.

The CIA had succeeded in a pilot study that involved making UK's M16 subservient to the CIA. From then on, the US political group at one hand leads global political elites whilst the US Intel Agencies lead other nations' intelligence bodies – bingo for the Washington *schemers*. Furthermore, such undertaking set off the US military involvement in foreign coups d'état and rebellions dabbed 'civil' wars. To this day, the US spy agencies and their subcontractors (sometimes very small, formless but extremely skilled contingents and special cells an insider has had his pen writing about in the book *"Confessions of an Economic Hit Man"*) are leading elements in regime changes and economic 'gigs' globally. Regime changes is not done for strategic reasons alone, it is a lucrative business as well.

The foregoing would finally become an addiction.

That addiction has made America – just like old Rome was – to continue earning steady hatred. The danger is, increasing global awareness of her manoeuvres is cause for alarm. If one bothers to study the world, one discovers steady shifts in people's views and what to expect from America and the West at large. One learns, sadly, that the 'world' is throwing in the towel. That is to say, the world is accepting America as an undefeated and unmatched power in world history. That was the import of Muammar Gaddafi's last words to Libyans. Gaddafi decried that he was being fought by the biggest military power ever has been on earth. The same impression features in Obama's Cairo speech. In that eloquent piece Obama alludes to America being 'the power and reality of world greatness ever'.

Close examination of Chinese and Russian policies today reveal increasing forms of 'appeasement', 'compromise' and 'subtle' fears of the USA. For example, the two are now overtly cowering from opposing America's belligerent global policies and outlooks. Somehow they are even betraying their old time allies to avoid America's wrath. Recently (in 2018) the two snubbed North Korea on crucial issues and compromised over Syria's sovereignty, peace and autonomy. The ex-communists went almost mute over Iran's tension with Donald Trump.

It would seem that every other nation is scared of the USA. Or has wishes of pleasing her.

Some European nations for example are in each war the US initiates – be it rational or irrational as per their *own* people's views and laws. They remember George Bush's warning, 'you are either with us or against us'. They see no middle ground. Thus they vote for every decision and laws the US props up – this, a matter in records. For the last three decades, many sovereigns in Europe have lost autonomy in *some* policy, legal and diplomatic issues of international character. They second all the views put on the table by the USA. They are 'apprentices' of the USA in ways more than one.

Therefore, despite her failing internal affairs, America is going strong outside. In short, she has international glories at the expense of internal confusion. Dear readers, majority empires of the past came to their last in this way.

An Old Wisdom

This old wisdom, 'deal good, think twice' is still phenomenal. Many imperial smartasses suffered it. 'Being smart dares getting outsmarted' – this is natural. It is a primordial ego known of humans. For example, history lacks records of empires getting fought and successful defeated before they had basked in glories (good deals, failing to think twice). Not before those powers had had enough to boast of and think they are the smartest. I could find none. The reverse is almost always true. That empires first get good deals of their policies and reap too much out of their articulation. Empires become scourges to the outsiders because they primarily grow 'deadly' acquisitive. This behaviour becomes an addiction as wealth peaks. But wealth makes the wealthy full of themselves. And with wealth at megalomaniac stages arrogance creeps in, brazenly. Brutality and bluntness that ensues from such arrogance is what invites empire downfall. Because arrogance is irrational and is one of the most enduring human weaknesses. How is this possible in a sophisticated society? Let say an elitist society like the USA? The answer is simple.

When rich hegemons are hated and coveted by outsiders they almost universally become senseless. Wealth dulls the sense of those who own it. As I noted earlier, the haves are full of themselves and commit mistakes only 'bullies' delight in. They also 'overlook' the fact that they were able to rise, go out and conquer other lands because their 'people' stood tall and strong besides the rulers. This knowledge flop leads to an outward looking 'power logic' and love of political outlooks entirely disconnected from 'the people'. In a nutshell an empire becomes oriented and disoriented by external events. To some extent an empire's supremacy is assured of her power by holding-down other nations (those in proximity and across the shores) or other regions. By this time an empire's 'citizens' are partly forgotten (they become politicians' doormat) and their 'sweat' becomes supplementary to the goings. This is because for economic ends, *surely,* the outside is tenfold or more profitable than the small core population called 'citizens'.

The world is always greener than *a* country. When empires arrive at this discovery or recognition, are already walking downhill. This because such reasoning (coveting the world at the expense of 'intra-territorial' wellbeing) is doomed. Isn't the US here yet? Isn't the US now more attracted with the world and its huge resources than it reverts to cater for Americans? Go and inquire. I just made simple your homework.

And I am going to simplify that more in the next part...

...in the Last Days of America's Hegemony (17)

The Argead Dynasty Of Macedonia

The state of Macedonia under the Argead family (700 – 309BC) had been able to grow incrementally because her once humble royalty was able to concentrate on building internal strength.

The Macedonians, not outsiders (however rich outsiders are) were the target. Primary activities of the State involved developing the citizens, taking control of regional geographical advantages, ingraining wider scholarships amongst the people and elevating her position and grip on regional trade networks connecting the Aegean, the Mediterranean and beyond. This, amongst others, involved a strict policy of self-preservation: building prominent local identity, building people based prosperity and transforming the archipelago into successful commercial cities e.g. Vergina (Aegean), Pella, Amydon, Anthemus, Atalanta and others. The Argeads very much loved their Greek heritage and they championed for it.

The Argeads believed in investing in human development – spurring the Macedonians to realise more values from their labour and to earn respect of the neighbouring polities that dotted the Greek islands. First, know that at one time Greeks had been cheap labourers and slave market of Persia. That was during the time Greeks were fragmented into tiny polities no larger than walled cities. With the leadership of the Argeads, Macedonians improved their value and status. A status based mainly on building a unified Greek identity. After asserting their self-worth and wider Greek identity Macedonians united in purpose, direction and motivation. Labour, which was now focused towards community growth, uplifted them. The true secret to people's success is making their labour focused onto themselves. Macedonians had no democracy but a monarchy through which kings ensued. The people prospered because the king lived and worked for them. Always working hard to remove his people from servitude, drudgery and foreign abuse. They had been vassals at one time in the past so the kings knew well how vassalage hurt.

Macedonians would prosper for centuries until problems came, starting from within. The trouble arrived when she had resoundingly progressed, and an ambitious king took power. This man was first of all a guardian of an infant heir – he wasn't, as per tradition, destined to be king. He usurped the crown. The throne under wrong buttocks. The man was Phillip II. Phillip ruled between 360 – 336BC after his brother, king Perdiccas III, was killed in battle. Yes, Phillip proved capable for the job and underwent extensive transformation of the Greek lives. But he unsuspectingly crossed the often necessary but redline of power contours. That is the growth in fighting capability. Which means, 'revolutionising' the Army.

I have in the course of studying ancient and modern histories of power – civilisations and empires included – come to reckon with the fact that when strong polities innovate their 'Armies', trouble knock on the door. Armies, however sophisticated they get, are instruments of death. They are meant for killing. So it was in Babylonia long ago (under Gen. Nabupolassar and his son, Gen. Nebuchadnezzar II), Elam, Persia, Rome, Mongolia (the Khan dynasty) and others. The US is the course's modern retainer. It takes few decades for a military might to turn arrogant and start self-destroying – often through endless warring and scheming.

By the time King Phillip II strengthened the Macedonian Armies, making regionally formidable hosts, he planned warring against non-Greeks and neighbours. The leading combat innovation he had devised, and that carried the day, was introduction of 'phalanxes' in an otherwise common battle formation. The square block (phalanxes) of solidly locked infantry men was extremely effective that no contemporary rivals could match. It was an innovation far ahead of its time. It would wait long for the Roman formation of legions to outdo it. With that surety of power arrogance set in and with wealth, Pella could face any polity standing in her way. Note this: the more military prowess Macedonia gathered the more ambitious (and confident) her generals became. This boiling culminated into the worst the region could get. For example, Macedonian generals remembered and retold each slight Greeks had suffered for hundreds of years. The narratives mobilized for revenge... Shows of military powers actually. They had no pushes or pulls to start wars but mere *memories*.

The seething got frenzy when King Phillip II died in some suspicious circumstances and his hot-blooded generals got hold of his son – the heir Alexander III – later famous as Alexander the Great. The heir was offhand first thing. He had suffered a raft of childhood frustrations, stresses, fear of being side stepped (unrecognised) amongst the royalties and all that. Being from a fiercely polygamous family (his mother was the fourth wife of Phillip II) Alexander had been raised in a climate of family competitions and treacheries for the king's attention. A life full of sly moves, deceptions and manipulations. Sort of risky upbringing. An upbringing wherein one had to take his chance. Hadn't he a *scheming* mother – Olympias – he would have ended up an alcoholic that he was. Would have ended a young, heavy drinker or a victim of family assassination. But Olympias was an iron lady, she saw to it that her son got what *she* wanted. In some reports it is written that *possibly* the queen schemed for 'murder' of her husband to secure the kingship for the son.

He was tender – twenty years possibly – when Alexander sat on the throne at Pella. The Greek wealth and military powers he inherited got in his head immediately founding an idealist. And all that after grim bloodshed. A story of an emotional, day-dreaming prince Alexander's is. He visited a tomb(s) presumed to be Achilles' and thought he would emulate the mythical warrior. The Persian conqueror of the old, Cyrus II, appealed to Alexander's impulse and again he dreamed to win wars like the Persian. There came idealism, ideas and ideas... Ones that would take him across river Styx at a mere 32 years.

The story of Alexander III sickens if told candidly – with a hint of psychological analysis. Though when retold with an emotional fanfare it sounds great. The two approaches are quite different. Alexander was a victim of political forces bigger than him. Forces well known in politics of power... Forces that have made kings do things they never thought. Almost *constantly* the heads of empires are victims/are manipulated of/by the aristocrats and the courtiers. Alexander suffered this earnestly.

Today you hear, when it cannot be concealed any more, US Presidents admitting of having been fouled by advisors: legal staffs, economic strategists, PR consultants and top diplomats. Listen president Donald Trump repeatedly pick on John Bolton as 'warmonger'. What do you make of that? Me: that he has been creeping under the president's skin - always pressuring for a fight. Bolton, John *et al* make up the first and closest power players. And no smart president can avoid their net. In the old days, the *courtiers* spun such deals. Military and security advisors have over history been the worst scammers repeatedly misleading the executives to strategies beyond the commanders-in-chief ever needed. Many wars were/are projections top security 'advisors' put on the table *not* deliberations put forward by rational public entities. Herein one learns who actually make wars. In Pella long time ago Alexander III fell victim of this reality. His generals, courtiers and wealthy nobilities (majority reputed ex-warriors) worked crisscrossing ambitions. They outsmarted the young man (based on the prince's naivety) sending him to spend himself warring. The old men remained in Pella hunting and accumulating more wealth at his back. And when he was declared dead (ignobly and surrounded by a highly divided, exotic Army) the old men took power easily. This, of course, included slaughtering his would be heir – Alexander's own son Alexander IV. Truly mercilessly that was.

And that was the end of the Argead dynasty. The end of a family full of luminous aristocrats. The end of the Macedonian Empire... The so called Hellenisation (spreading Greek culture and lifeways far and wide) was murdered by a boy king who died in a strange land surrounded by a horde of strangers. He had grown too bold as to trust his life with mercenaries, total passers-by. He had forgotten he was carrying the destiny of his people with him. And since his death the Greeks have never risen their back. Sad. Poor Greece.

The Wars Of Alexander The Great

Not too much can be learned from Macedonia's imperialism and Alexander's wars to buttress my thesis on America in the days of waning. Yet the few available are so convincing I couldn't let go.

First, Macedonia's exploits are proof that having strong militaries – however good that sounds – is a problem. Strong militaries mentor political arrogance. Powerful militaries have over histories been destroyers of civilizations. We see even today, the more the US Army sophisticates the more insecure the world becomes. The US Army is always manipulating this or that to set the world in fear of war(s). Yet that takes tolls from Americans themselves, in the end.

Second, with wealth and military powers Alexander went to conquer the world. America does exactly that using her huge wealth and strong Air Force to replay history's déjà vu. And this began one April 1917.

Third, when Alexander went outside to grow from 'boy king' to 'lord of hosts' – in the footsteps of his idol, Cyrus II of Persia, Pella and Macedonia ceased to be his orientation. The king saw the world for what it is: bigger, greener, lucrative! Once one tries it, one cannot turn back. Not even the mighty Cyrus II came back home alive - the world simply had become too big for him. Likewise, Alexander went on fighting outside wars for a decade plus and since then the throne (in Pella) remained unattended. He ruled through letters and correspondence! The capital retained and fell in the hands of the well-fed nobilities good at nothing but arguing, bickering, corrupting and idealising.

America's foreign preoccupations (like Macedonia's) have turned the US into an emporium and more of a lab. for tactical experiments. The USA is a workshop where the military, Intelligence agencies, security companies and politicians invent and practise techniques of coercion and global manipulations (Snowden's NSA leaks can give you a rough picture). The practices produce techniques US security and intelligence agencies are taking outside for regime changes. They are later useful tools for *psy-ops* at global scale.

The people in USA are again made the leading market for global technologies and consumables – this because they have the highest disposable income and by extension good purchasing power. They are reduced into dreamers who fantasize that wealth is the truest of prosperity and key to personal fulfilment (like Macedonian nobilities believed then). Looked at through analytical lenses, the US is headquarter of the spirit of 'ACQUISITIVENESS' – a spirit that, sadly, tend to end up inhuman. No wonder there is now internal full fledged terrorism they call 'gun killings' or 'mass shooting' to hide its true nature. Well, it is terrorism.

But the US acquisitiveness is now *largely* brought in by massive resources resulting from foreign exploits.

Fourth, the results of Alexander's preoccupations (read: wars for Hellenisation), which led to the weakening of internal stability of the Greek lands, are exactly that of America's. That is, busy with foreign wars, manoeuvring, idealising, subordinating foreigners to America's policy frameworks and Empire building or democratising, America is domestically growing shaky. For example, she no longer have moral grounds to stop gun killings at home. Or ensure public security after guns are sold. She cannot manage her police departments to stop *racially inclined* killings and humiliation. Police racism, that is. And yet she is busy preaching and selling strategies for global peace and security. Morality is becoming elusive in the USA. The same moral shakiness happened in Macedonia when Alexander left it unattended.

An American President is *now* measured by how many successful foreign ambitions he pulls through. This is the way Pella's generals, nobilities and aristocrats measured the greatness of Phillip and Alexander.

Empires are funny.

Last: with many foreign lands to outmuscle, Macedonia betrothed terror and threats. Alexander's brutality preceded him, making lands far afield that heard him tremble. And thus seek ways to offer submission. Many people without knowledge of this history and the life of Alexander III do not know he largely survived and won wars because he was terror in all but a name.

The phalanxes were an unconquerable block – just like today's US Air Force is. And when Alexander defeated a polity he left streaming blood and gnawing sorrow in his wake. He spared very few adversaries and that only when it suited his tactics. Or his ego. Assassinations, poisoning and gruesome killings were his trademarks. For his love and prowess at killing, Alexander commanded and fought from the front. He was a king fighting his own battles. Macedonia was, in her heydays, feared for her use of terror and mercilessness. It was a bully of a hegemon that sent fear before the Armies marched.

I won't say that of America. Think it on your own. Get your answer. You better swallow that.

And never ever say I alluded to it.

Naturally, Humanly

Reading analyses, opinions and research outputs one learns many scholars (economists in a majority) think America's imperial decline will come from getting outdone/outperformed by a host of emerging economies. Some argue China, Russia, India and many others will in the long run see to that. There are others who, sometimes ago, proposed Japan would surpass the USA.

I refute that rather economic view of civilizations. History shows no such trends. Even with more recent examples, like the decline of Britain (?Europe) as a superpower to the ascent of USA. We do not see economic variables playing the leading role. History reveals that empires die from within.

The US ascended rapidly to clinch global hegemony when European powers struggled with internal (*inside*) crises which culminated into the First World War. That had nothing to do with economic machinations done by the US of A.

The powerful Soviet Union that *almost* took global hegemony after the Second World War hadn't it been for the USA, would prove the economy isn't much of a factor. I doubt the USSR had tough economic muscles enough to compete for over-all global command. Though I can readily see the USSR had a societal shape (human agency and other rational factors) that threatened to set her above the powers that be. They were the techniques used by the USA, amongst them, that of sabotaging the idea and place of socialism vis-a-vis human welfare that won the race.

And as you read backwards, you will find no empire ever fell out due to languishing economy. No. Maybe that could happen if internal problems manifested through economic weaknesses...

See, when politicians become belligerents, worshippers of stern militarism, burn of desires for wealth, bask in acquisitiveness and grow irrevocably immoral the decline is at hand. The psychology of power (the study of dynamics related to power control, especially its related mind-set) is sure to explain this very well. I just tried to elucidate this *psyche* with Alexander III of Macedonia. His selfish, arrogant, terrorising and scheming aristocrats first graduated into all those attitudes. And thus Macedonia went downhill.

King Phillip II and Alexander III share one psychological trait worthy a note. They were royalties born and raised in a respected hierarchy. They didn't grow in a struggling polity. They came of age within firmly rooted, rich kingdom. They had been happier kids with access to excesses. They could risk living their thoughts (dreams) and make gambles as much as kids from rich families gamble earlier on, using their families' wealth. Thus unlike Macedonia's founding Argeads who had been practical men, the last two kings were pure idealists. They knew what they wanted and moved to snatch it. And that, without enough caution. Their acts represent a nature well known in psychosocial studies and broadly explored in sociology of knowledge. That men born in luxuries, assurance, abundance and comfort are frequently carefree although they may look smart in face. They tend to make too many idiosyncratic decisions. They usually fail to master practical calculations – because they have an unconscious fear of defeat and humiliation.

The psychology I am referring to is well represented in the Greek mythology 'the fall of Troy' - as narrated in Homer's "*Iliad*". Greek kings gather tens of thousands of their finest to go fight (mostly die) because one of their own, a Greek king (Menelaus) just lost a beautiful wife, Helen. A young, supple queen who wants out because she has fallen in love with the 'girls' charmer, the master seducer Paris, prince of Troy. The story is a myth yet it fairly treats the absurd simplicity of people born in power and wealth.

In a society at large, people born in an environment of comfort (say: matured and stable economies) think their freedoms, liberal rights and democratic experiences are the most important things in life. They are very wrong. They count not the cost they pay for that happiness. Even when the happiness *presumed* good is actually destructive (or *enslaving* according to Plato).Costs like the thousands of warriors Greek kings went to sacrifice to punish Troy for the lass - queen Helen. Plato had a run for it...

Plato's Analyses: The Human Numbers

To explain why in powerful polities (like Athens) where people were well developed, rich and civilized there rose aristocrats not worth a damn, i.e. weak democrats, naïve nobilities, noisy Kings and sluggish princes etc. Plato wandered. He then offered a complex calculation leading to what he calls 'the *human numbers*'.

In that calculation Plato thinks that there are days, years and times for birth of good leaders. I insist: Plato says there is a time 'good, intelligent and able people' are conceived – not all the time. Again he says 'only people with the knowledge (of those numbers) can get the Maths correct and thus breed abled offspring'. The problem with many aristocrats, according to Plato, is that they don't know those 'numerical matches' and thus they cannot calculate well to sear intelligent offspring by using that numerical benefit. As a result of their ignorance of this fact, the aristocrats bear poor quality children (less intelligent ones) who later become pleasure ridden, ignoble, self-destroying and full of unnecessary desires.

Therein he gave explanation why 'down the line princes and aristocrats' (call them all: statesmen) tend to be less competent (less intelligent, less practical) in comparison to their predecessors. Plato notes this may happen to be different if a couple is favoured to strike successful coital union on the superb numbers – mostly by chance. This last explains why sometimes good leaders (and good people generally) may leave brilliant heirs after them. But chances are always not good.

Perhaps Plato is right. Maybe he is wrong. Who knows? After all, this world is full of mysteries and a lot of incomprehensible interrelations. He gave his damn and he is worthy of respect.

Whatever the case is, we know matter-of-factly, not many commendable leaders were/are lucky to have/leave similar heirs – although it may happen. Likewise, it is rare that bright communities ever leave similar offspring. The world has had this many a time that historians wonder what really happens. There are cases wherein a civilization(s) simply crumble and people degenerate into oblivion without sound explanations. A well-known example in this case would be the demise of the Mayan and Incan civilizations of Central America. Scholars (historians and archaeologists alike) still cannot exactly pinpoint what happened. The two cannot be sufficiently explained (as if they retreated into backwardness). Add the Old Zimbabwe Kingdom in Africa to that mystery.

In addition to those, one cannot explain how or why the solidly built Macedonia (full of great philosophers, strategists and visionary nobilities) could simply have fallen into a naïve kid's hands (Alexander III, tutored by the sage Aristotle himself) in a wave of terror and bloodletting. Alexander ascended after a wave of killings that shook the foundations of Pella itself. The true generals of the Macedonian Armies simply watched, unperturbed by the unfolding. Macedonians clapped hands for him. The whole Greek pride was to be ruined soon in a mere fifteen years of senseless fighting.

Again, if not for Plato's idea of the wobbling offspring down the line, how do you explain the folly that Gnaeus Pompey Magnus was able to lull Rome's highly trained, politically sensitive Senate into self-imposed exile? The rabid statesmen believed by abandoning Rome, they were being tactical enough. That they could hide afar and then surge back to defeat Julius Caesar.

I am caught grinning every time I read that story.

Caesar comes from some brave fighting in Gaul, at the head of a full host – well seasoned ranks and files that had had countless forays and major battles. Everyone in Rome is afraid. The Gaul veterans are with no match. Heavens are trembling, the gods are crying. For they had never before beheld such unfolding spectacle of imminent doom. But Pompey is clever to stand in the Senate House and say, 'you know what, gentlemen? I can best Caesar if you give me one last trust. We go together to Greece where my loyal legions are. There I will prepare my men and bolster them. In a year's time we should be able to come back and rout that son of a bitch, uh!' If the Senate hadn't what Plato calls a poor offspring, none would have wasted his time dreaming. No one would have wasted his lifetime following a sick general as if the Capitol would vanish due to the absence of a few hundred old men best in nothing than day long talkings. But then there was no Rome of the likes of Scipio Africanus (236 – 183BC). It was Rome of small men born on 'the other numbers'. Grandiloquent, yelping men who lived after pleasures – ones not ready to soil their fingers. Caesar gave them a treat.

Neither can one understand how Julius Caesar, a general empowered by sheer idealism and arrogance could have arm-twisted Rome's old, tested traditions to knock the Capitol to ruins.

Nor can one understand why citizens in most empires soon grow passive and resigned that in time they become too slow in thinking and cannot know danger when they see one…

An example today: the mushrooming sex dolls business and a host of technologies that enable a person to self-gratify sexually, are underlain with a need to do away with some nuisances related to cohabitation, marriage and interpersonal intimacy. The idea being that with one's own bought doll(s), one can be real free in everything on daily basis. One can use his own time-table without a woman to come back to – a woman to question why you are late. Or why you are making that call to a strange girl in the middle of the night. May be how you spend the money you earn and other issues. So, to do away with all that, one has that beautiful doll meant to look like Kim Kardashian. Kim's physique. Yet, a very servile doll – one you can fuck anyway you want and throw away naked or so, until next time you get an erection. One that awaits you not only at home (in the sense of a wide place) but exactly where you want (on a bed naked, maybe). And of course you meet her that time you choose. If it had been alive, that thing would be more than a slave. Even a puppy is better than that *woman*. Now see? This is a slow think-ing in its original sense. For it is a result of a society that liber-ally thought it needed full equality between men and women. That they could be equal to each other and clash eye to eye. Question each other and take each other to task. Tolerating no misgivings – they thought.

Well that sounds good and I love it. But the idea underlying sex dolls is an insult to that thought. It loudly says people still need servile partners. Or at least one that doesn't make things deeply strained as are gender rights today. Partners are shying away (running away) from the equality the society intellectually thought is a good thing. Equality has destroyed natural intimacy (the emotional, illogical, unconditional love) and is scaring many out of wedlock. Some are afraid of marrying or committing to full interpersonal relationship. They need back that woman or that man who can sit back ready to get lain anytime, anywhere they want. Not this current partnership climate frequently infested with 'too much knowing' that many homes are psychological labs.

Sum up all the above...

At the least we learn there is an element of societal weakness that precedes downfall. That powers grow and when they attain the highest level possible for civilizations (in their time) rulers immerse in unnecessary desires (here Plato is right). There arrives a time pleasure seeking becomes so stubborn all that people think of is happiness, freedom, grandeur, recklessness and sheer irresponsibility. They demand and do whatever can bring pleasure - they don't care the price in the now or eventually. Pleasured lives become soft and irresponsible.

In précis, there is born a society in which anything goes. At this point the society has weak men who live for pleasantries and a population more foolish, sadistic and dumb compared to its hard-working predecessors. Politicians become hollow minds. Politics degenerate into pettiness. Yes, the wrangling tea-parties...

That is the last of their mistakes...

...in the Last Days of America's Hegemony (18)

"**A**merica should know that peace with Iran is mother of all peace and war with Iran is the mother of all wars" – Hassan Rouhani, president of the Islamic Republic of Iran (22nd July 2018).

The moment I heard those words I couldn't help but smile. Superficially, they don't seem to have much weight because against the USA Iran is a small nation with an even smaller military capacity, fewer weaponry, inadequate human and technological intelligence and a limited budget. All facts of practical necessity and expediency considered, Iran shouldn't be shouting back. The USA can break Iran's back in 1001 ways. However, historically inquired, the words take us further. I cannot pinpoint what the president meant though. Amongst others he had started with, "Mr Trump, don't play with the lion's tail, this would only lead to regret".

Loaded words they are, mh! I didn't know Rouhani was that good in rhetoric.

The Middle East, The Graveyards Of World Empires

Rouhani's threats take us back to what Iran has been and her immense contribution to the modern world. That is, Iran has history. A good thing is in his speech the president alludes to history and Iran's political maturity. All of them true in history. The US knows how resilient the Persians (Iranians of the Old) were. Plain though the words sound, they are a people not to be shrugged off and ignored. Many a civilization have had their graveyards dug in and near the desert of old Persis.

That region is infamous for death of empires. I give few examples here: one, the Babylonian Empires (classical and neo-Babylonians) famed for their luminaries who outfought the old world, met their death on crossing to Elam – the old name used by some Iranians before Persia. By 539BC the last strong empire in Mesopotamia, one that had been strengthened by the Chaldeans, was decimated by Cyrus the Great when he toppled Nabonidus. The havoc caused by Cyrus marked the end of Babylonia to this day. Cyrus was a Persian General as you will soon learn.

Two, the Hellenistic Empire – that is the dominance Alexander of Macedonia was trying to make – ended at a few sand dunes away from the desert neighbouring Persis. Alexander succumbed to a strange disease not known until now. I tend to suspect 'the disease' was a result of cumulative impact of various, alcoholically indeterminate, portent brews he had been gulping for a decade plus.

Three, the Roman Republic amongst other reasons had her critical moment blocked by the Parthian 'bulls' of the old – when Gen. Marcus Licinius Crassus and his son Gen. Publius and their legions (thirty thousand well trained Romans) were decimated at Carrhae (that is Abraham's old home known as Harran, in the field of Paddan Aram). And that is few hills away from old Persis. The death of Crassus c. 53BC, one of the power stoppers in Rome (he was one of the figures of an alliance known then as the first triumvirate, and possibly the richest man in Rome) gave free sway to Caesar and Pompey – the first known destroyers of old Rome.

There is more examples.

Iran is the sociological mother of world civilizations. No single area throughout history has contributed too much. Iran was the pioneer and architect of a strong, vast empire – as big as a million square miles – subjecting hundreds of languages and communities. Iran built the first biggest empire ever to survive longer in world history – for over 200 years. That is the Persian Empire based at Persis and Media. To date (2020) the US hegemony is barely a hundred years old.

Well, Iran is in fact the 'saviour' of the Jews. Iranians are the people who not only saved Jews from a raging captivity in Babylonia but also the ones who gave back to Jews their religion (the Jewish traditions now called Judaism). The Jewish Tanach and the Christian Bible (Isaiah 45:1-3) call the son of Iran – Cyrus II – a Messiah (God's anointed one). That is a very special accolade in the Jewish orthodox sense. Although today we see full Jewish arrogance against Iranians/increased Zionist hatred of the Islamic Republic in Tehran, history says the Jews as a people owe their survival to Persians. No one is sure the Jews would be who they are today if a noble Persian hadn't scaled his ambitions to see to that. Who knows? The Jews were captives in Babylonia. And subsequent to their captivity the King who took them – Nebuchadnezzar – had grown mentally deranged! He could as well had them slaughtered to sooth his daemons.

Yes, there are tens of ethnic groups contemporary to Jews who disappeared in circumstances far less serious than captivity e.g. the Jebusites, Canaanites, Amorites, Philistines etc. All we know is that in the end it took the Persian statesman for the Jewish God, Yahweh, to save the Jews.

Cyrus Ii And The History Of Power

In Persis (modern day Fars, a bit off the City of Shiraz) a son was born. A boy who would bequeath a lot to this world. His name was Cyrus II – a prince of Persia (old Anshan) – son of Cambyses I (600–559BC). Cyrus was born in a fast growing kingdom and was lucky to find his Achaemenes dynasty (705–329BC) had built strong armies. Troubles – as always throughout empires – begin with possession of strong armies. Cyrus (580–529BC) took the military and wealth Persians had toiled for to go forth conquering Media, Lydia and Babylonia. His idealism had just begun. An idealism that first sealed fate to what Nebuchadnezzar II (605–562BC) – the skilful Chaldean prince and the able general of the Babylonian armies – had made of the Mesopotamia and its surroundings. Appetites for wars once an empire is in gears do not end with victories. They trudge on. That held steadfastly with Cyrus II (the first man in history given the epithet, 'The Great'). He warred on and on until death took him in surprise.

Cyrus fought nasty wars conquering a vast area. He subdued lands in the East, West and North of Mesopotamia and exploited every living creatures in his way. He was an able general to begin with. Yet he was capable of the wins as long as his Army remained stronger and growing – as is a rule for Empire survival. In an Empire militarism is an addiction. To the end of his life (529BC) Cyrus would leave an Empire so cruel, so terrorizing and hell-bent to crash any renegade. Neighbours alike. The whole region had become a field of war, a bloodspot. His son, the heir Cambyses II, would further expand the Empire conquering Egypt.

Through his war experience Cyrus saw, as an eye opener, that power corrupts the more it grows. He saw himself becoming absolute. Saw that the use of his powers buoyed his ego. He saw as well that this phenomenon threatened endless rebellions amongst the conquered territories. This, despite the fact wars were presenting to Persians an over-lordship of immense degree. Exercising an over-lordship taught Cyrus *how* subduing many lands at a go was costly and unsustainable. He thus did the smartest algebra of power operations. The *risks* manifest out of those algebraic operations pushed him towards invention of the pillars of *modern* politicisation – adoption of political tactics and quick adaptation of the same to practical necessities. He created and reformulated some new forms of politics not based entirely at the centre. The advent of decentralisation, that was. See? Decentralisation was born as a practical necessity... long ago in Persia.

Allies had to be created and made to remain in the vicinity; so, Cyrus first made the famous 'edicts of restoration'. As the name suggests the edicts restored what had been there in the first place but had been thwarted this or that way by preceding 'bully' states before him. One, previously conquered lands were to be returned to their former 'lords'. That is, the local rulers recovered their former powers thus diffusing their tensions with the King in Persis. He in fact recalled the old versions of politics in the peripheries. The subjects were to rule themselves under the Persian pervasive kingship (subjects became autonomous states exercising internal self-rule as they say today) as long as they paid tributes.

His tactics were underlain by a show of being kind to his subjects. He could even move to fight a rebellious chief for the sake of a neighbour who had extended his hand – accepting the lordship of Persia. The lesser lords (now very mean) under him were called 'Satraps'. Two, he restored the cultures of his subjects (even captives) making it legal to exercise one's identity and religion. Sometimes he even pledged allegiance to other people's supreme deities. It was in these 'outsmarting' political calculations that the Jews got lucky. Their culture was wholesomely restored. Their Judaism was reborn. Actually Cyrus was even prepared to go as far as giving the Jews a new temple in Jerusalem. He knew diplomacy very well. The Jews were, atop all that, let loose to go back home – read the Tanach. Cyrus was a great statesman.

Today, America's global power stays are the military bases. Camps spread widely amongst lands of allies and some remote areas. Well, that is a tried and failed mechanics of imperial control. None had it figured better than Cyrus II. He was, roughly speaking, the founder. To disrupt rogue entities under the Satraps (puppets-cum-allies) Cyrus made sure no one else had strong militaries. He foiled any such attempts. All over the Persian Empire spotted were Persian military forts ready to deploy and crash rebellions – timely, mercilessly and efficiently. Their orders were to make sure Persian imperialism remained ripe everywhere and functional. The camps were vigilantes.

To this day this is how imperial powers (see the USA) deploy over swathes of lands under foreign allies. The military bases 'psychology' that America is famous of takes a leaf from failed Persian mechanics. It's a 'phantom'. It's a 'has been'.

In Persia Long Time Ago

If we learn from deeds than words – because actions speak louder – we have got a school in what Cyrus the Great (and his Achaemenes dynasty) did than reading Greek, British and American philosophies of power.

The Achaemenes lived the pioneering phase of human history of running vast states. States of multivariate communities wherein power was coveted, feared and tricky to maintain. The dynasty is collegiate.

Cyrus II et al ruled when 'humanity' still delighted in heroism. People in those days famed bloodshed, martyrdom and sacrifice. They ululated wars, legends, epic myths and believed in strength. Wars raged on as if they were rites of passage. Men lived in constant loggerheads and killed each other with wantonness. If a young man reached a prescribed age for maturity he had to prove his manhood. As a matter of decorum he would have to kill an 'out-folk(s)', decapitate him/them and boast of their heads. They called it, in some communities, making one's bones (read: one became a grown man because he had showed he could kill others). Families thus had a treasure of bones to remember and prove their sons had successfully earned their manhood! Those bones were kept safe as one today keeps safe her academic transcripts.

A long time ago patriotism that communities enshrined would '*outright*' scare the hell out of us. It was for instance usual for one community to annihilate another only to grab one's resource patch. And those acts meant being patriotic to one's own people (the killers). Perhaps now you see when and how patriotism *through* killing became a noble act. War was a means to an end whereas fear was the biggest ally to mail to a neighbour. The world was dark indeed.

There was a time in human history fear was an asset. Powers schemed and manoeuvred to infuse fear amongst the people. Real or perceived fear – whatever that could work. Acts that prove this are traced in almost all gone empires throughout history. Those acts were precursors to several strands of modern terrorism. Plains were fields of swords and bloodshed. Empires were maintained by the edge of daggers, poisons... and arrows. Many days were full of bloodshed and sorrow... A sizeable percentage of children in all communities were sure to be raised orphans before they themselves (most likely) went to create the next line of orphans...

Cyrus of Persia attempted to correct all those. And through that win his subjects...

So Cyrus initially worked for and became founder of a host of 'human rights'. First, he allowed the people to believe in whatever they liked and *freely* exercise their religious dogma. Gods had been bones of contention, he made them irrelevant to that cause. Implied therein is, he was purveyor of secularism. No way could a leader allow 'diversity' of faiths in his polity if the state took side(s). He didn't give himself the quality of divinity either. He exemplified respect for 'community-others' by liberating captives that were held in all lands he conquered. The Jews recorded this with exultation. Second, Cyrus allowed foreigners (the poor and the learned individuals) to traverse Persia for greener pastures – thus making his polity the first global *economy* in history. Records obtained in Persepolis after its fall reveal the first ever structured system of employment and paid jobs appeared in this period. That is, the first creation of paid labour. Ancient Greeks recorded this. Greeks were the leading labourers in Persia this time.

When an empire is so fertile it has its economic lushness turning the core into greener pastures. People from deprived peripheries migrate to 'the nucleuses' of the bigger economy to pluck pastures. Often, migrants first settle as cheap labourers but soon cope to become an industrious lot. This is not a hallmark of humanity just today (in USA and Europe where migrants are flocking). So it was from time immemorial. The Persian Empire, for example, had her greener metropolises crawling with cheap, industrious immigrants e.g. Persépolis, Pasargadae, Ecbatana, Susa and Babylonia eventually were awash with incomers. The present Arab elements in Iran, as we know it today, start in this period – as trekkers migrating to work and earn a living.

Traditions have it that Greek noble classes were at one time recognized based on how fair individuals had assimilated the Persian elements of *souci*, life style, elegance and sophistication. In their homes, pre-Hellenistic Greeks narrated with awe the virtues, good wills and blessedness of the Persian nobilities. This is how Alexander the Great would become delighted with the life, time and deeds of Cyrus II (Greeks called him Cyrus the Elder). From his young age, Alexander III dreamt of becoming a Cyrus II. Cyrus was his role model and the boy grew talking of his virtues and greatness. He would later live to emulate (at least in courage and war fighting) the conqueror. This he personally *admitted* in later years as a successful general.

Having introduced Satraps all over the Persian dominions, the Achaemenes successfully invented an indirect rule or else say they concealed the puppetry system. Therein we get the essence of allies and puppets. Allies are puppets. For at play between each of the two and their guarantor is an 'undue influence'. An influence in which the stronger use the weaker. The enduring mechanism used to retain this is through 'spying on and disrupting' the plans of the ally. This surely sounds more or less playing puppetry.

Mazidaysm and/or Zoroastrianism became, frankly speaking, the Persian mails to the world. They converged in Judaism, Christianity and Islam. Mazidaysm invented 'monotheism'- the belief in one great god – Ahura Mazda. And it contributed many other elements now raised high in Judaism, Christianity and Islam. Some such elements are today's foundations of political manoeuvres. For example, 'day of judgment' believed in the three Abrahamic religions (Judaism, Christianity and Islam) is Zoroastrian. It is a black fear of the unknown (afterlife) that has made millions subservient to illusions. Illusions politicians use to abuse humanity. It says that one day (presumed the last day, *al Qiyamah*) each and every one of us is going to be answerable for her deeds - all of us, the living and the dead.

In Judaism, Christianity and Islam words 'lord of lords', 'lord of hosts', 'king of kings' and hundreds of attributes given to God are virtues first bestowed (based on existing records) on Cyrus the Elder. Perhaps they are from afar, even before Persia. They might be from Sumerians, Akkadians or Egyptians. Well, who knows? Civilizations seem to be sprints, giving batons.

It isn't *cul-de-sac.*

Muslims: Meet Dhul Al Qarnayn

Islam's Qur'an (Surah Al Kahf 83 – 98) and some other traditions believed to be true (*sahih*) have a narrative of an enigmatic king who is pious and merciful he is not of this earth. The verses describe a victorious king who is so special in deeds that his good will, virtues, exploits and beliefs are transcendental. As usual, the book's narratives are credited to Allah's own revelation – he is the one telling his prophet to say the story (verse 83) of this blessed servant of *his* to the followers of Islam (the *umma*).

Allah, the one God of Islam, doesn't tell the actual name of the king. Instead Muhammad talks of 'the king in possession of'– the words *Dhul al Qarnayn*. The identity is strange, really questionable. And it cannot be a person's name. Its meaning in English would be something close to 'possessor *(dhul)* of two horns *(qarnayn)*. Its meaning does outright suggest of possession i.e. a king (lord) who had/possessed two horns – possessor of two horns (or the lord of two horns).

One is in privilege to know more about this narrative on reading Abdullah Yusuf Ali's interpretation (*tafsir*) of the Qur'an. He runs a great discourse (he calls it a commentary) trying to identify the possible king being exulted by the book. Yusuf Ali eventually ends up naming the possessor as 'Alexander the Great'. That proposal creates many questions than answers it provides. It is a great failure that overlooks a lot of known historical facts about 'horns' and their allusion. There have been scholars disputing him since. Although there are many others who supported the hypothesis before and after that *tafsir*.

What the Qur'an provides about this exceptional ruler-conqueror is that he was a great, noble king. He was real mighty yet one benevolent man who went about spreading mercy to his people, his subjects and all who met him seeking justice. In some instances, he helps lesser tribes (chiefs) subdue their enemies because the defeated chiefs, like Dhul Qarnayn himself, believe in *one great god* and the *day of judgement*. The lord who possessed two horns, according to the Qur'an, fought wars in three directions expanding his empire far and wide. His were victories bestowed to him by the almighty Allah.

Analysis: The king being said in the Qur'an is obviously Cyrus II of Persia – Cyrus the Great. The break in simple connectives that would guarantee easy identification of the Qur'an 'possessor of two horns' are mainly to blame on the way the story of Cyrus reached Arabia – the Hejaz and eventually Muhammad the prophet. It arrived through the Iraq connection – the narratives that had spread in Mesopotamia after the fall of Babylon.

Archaeologists can quickly figure out why horns feature on a king's head as 'possession'. It is that a long time ago, around the Mesopotamia, the animal horns' crescent-like form was used in the likes a hallo was regarded by Christians. Following this idea of metaphor, in English there is an allusion to "the horns of a crescent". By the way, Muhammad was preaching in the seventh century after Christ. The story of Cyrus II is of a ruler who lived in the sixth century before Christ – a thousand plus years apart. Again, the people who recycled the ruler's virtues in the Hejaz – to the seventh century AD - didn't receive the story as a historical lesson rather as a narrative already filled with sagas and admiration.

The Jews Cyrus liberated from the Babylonian captivity had lived to tell lofty stories similar to Muhammad's. And some of their descendants later settled in Yathrib – modern day Medinah al-Nabi (they were the Jews of Khaybar and *Banu* Qurayza. There were at least three more groups). Associated with these Jews there is an often 'suppressed' story you can find in the works of some writers. A story hinting that most likely, Muhammad himself had Jewish heritage. He had at least one of his direct maternal grandparents who was a Jew!

Other studies add that outside Palestine there had been no bigger Jewish settlements than those in Yathrib before and by the time of the prophet Muhammad. Even the name *'medinah'* (precedes Muhammad for centuries) is Jewish Aramaic. For Jews were the founders of the walled/fort cities of Yathrib which they called 'medinas' - i.e. the cities. The current Saudi Arabian city called Medina al- Nabi was a predominant Jewish settlement.

Those Jews are the narrators Muhammad was in contact with in the early years of his prophethood – and some scholars think the great part of what Muhammad preach related to Torah and the Tanach originated with the narratives he received from those Jews.

Historians know well that after a hero is gone or an event has transpired narrators tend to sensationalise and mystify him/ it over time. In the long run, all that remains of the natural events and sequence are inundated with exaggerations and biases based on whether the narrators hate, admire or are neutral to the personality (in history, ethnographers work hard to detect this infection). The mystification explains for example why as per the Qur'an narrative the king was a Muslim (although we know, matter-of-factly, Islam never existed before Muhammad). Again the hero (Dhul Qarynayn) is a believer in the day of judgement and one who affirms to one 'great god' proclaimed in Islam (Allah the Great, Allah Akbar) (note: *Akbar* = great).

Yes, Dhul al Qarnayn is Cyrus II if one applies historical facts to decipher the story. First, the perceived 'two horns' was a common symbol of exultation (representing the moon's crescent shape) in Mesopotamia. When one was admired and looked upon in awe, the people in that area drew him with some reverence showing wisdom and eminence and this was represented by two horns of a bull on his head. Alexander III got this honour, yes. Over time the horns would be drawn differently (varying directions) yet their origin is well known to archaeologists and historians studying ancient Mesopotamia. Horns were symbols to indicate reverence of the god Nanna – the god of moon and wisdom. Subsequent to that, any great statesman regarded as possessing wisdom (and better judgement) shared Nanna's holy horns of the crescent moon.

The Qur'an doesn't mean having biological horns, the verses strictly mean possessing them. And yes there is a metaphor in Mesopotamia that alludes to 'the horn of a kingdom' to mean the 'power of a polity'. Now, here is where it becomes easier to identify Dhul al Qarnayn. The earliest king in that area to possess two horns, that is, to possess two horns of polities at a go (he was the king of Media and of Persia at the same time – the two horns) was Cyrus II. This went on like that as his virtues spread wide before he expanded his hold further afield. It is at this time (of possessing two kingships) that he was known as 'the lord of two horns'. That is what he entered Babylonia possessing, and popularly known of, when he liberated the Jews. And at this very time Jews exited Babylonia, leaving with the memory of a king who had two kingdoms in his fold.

It is true neighbouring chieftains had built a custom of going to Cyrus II for counsel and submission, seeking his protection. He was regarded wiser and of good counsel. Others asked him to help subdue their enemies - in effect they offered to be his satraps. This time's legends are *obviously* what reached Muhammad and appealed to him for his teachings.

You must also note that in most drawings, especially after the Neo-Babylonian period, Cyrus the Great is depicted in flapping wings – see at the back of the cover of this book. That spoke glorification of his person - a hint of divine regard. It is an open secret that *then* people regarded him angelically – a six winged seraph! That suggests divinity.

With the issue of allusion to two horns settled, every other piece of the story of Dhu al Qarnayn falls in place. I have presented above the incomparable virtues of Cyrus II and his tact. Amongst them that he was benevolent and some wars he fought simply to win favours of his subjects – these are what the Qur'an calls helping those who were mistreated. I also show that he was a nasty general on the battle field who won almost each battle he fought. That is what the Qur'an says as well. He was pious, well, whether you read the bible (Jews) or Xenophon (a Greek soldier telling how Greeks revered Cyrus) they both agree he was an honourable man. Jews crossed their depth to call him the anointed of YAHWEH – effectively making him the only non-Jew with that quality.

Xenophon writes about the fall of Persepolis (Persis) narrating the shock Greeks fell in when they heard their king – Alexander the Great – had *coldly* burnt the city Cyrus had commissioned as his Empire's headquarter. According to Xenophon they were horrified and ashamed, unbelieving any sensible man would dare burn the great Persepolis – the city was to them synonymous to Cyrus the Elder. Alexander took a long time to convince Greeks it was necessary to burn Persepolis to avenge the torching of the Acropolis of Athens. Persians had burned the city of Athens in 480BC when they fought the Greeks during the second Greco-Persian War.

In short, if the Qur'an means a ruler so beloved and humble – it means Cyrus II.

I am not the first to argue Dhul al-Qarnayn was Cyrus II. Yet according to some scholars – mostly Muslim teachers and religious historians including Abdullah Yusuf Ali, Dhul al Qarnayn was Alexander the Great. Reading their works I accuse them of the tradition to be picky. That is, to carelessly choose Alexander because the latter is *more* famous and good to have in fold as a believer in Allah - a Muslim they claim he was! That is careless.

That is fanaticism. Alexander the Great was simply barbaric in his acts. He was a hell of an alcoholic who did a lot, like killing his own Generals, in fits of drunkenness. Far be humility from him. He was a dead harlot whose army carried with it thousands of paid prostitutes to satisfy soldiers. Even comparing Alexander and Caesar (in terms of virtues) would be comparing 'dawn' and the 'afternoon'.

The burning of the magnificent Persepolis was instigated by Alexander's personal prostitute, Thais, who ambushed his conscience when the king was in utter drunkenness. It is reported that when he came off drunkenness and saw what he had done Alexander regretted and was horrified. He then quickly moved on to Pasargadae (a few miles from the burnt capital) where Cyrus II is buried and visited his idol's tomb in reverence – in what some scholars think was a rare show of regrets. The grave was two hundred years old when Alexander visited. Remember Alexander was a fan of Cyrus and had taken him as role model. He paid full homage. Alexander then commanded Aristobulus to care for the tomb (make repair and refit) and make sure it survived and was well protected. Aristobulus would document this in generous terms.

Again this Alexander III had groups of Army officers and ranks and files who exercised vicious public homosexuality. They were known as 'the boy lovers'. Alexander came from a pantheon full of gods. And Greeks in his time believed death was crossing a black river called Styx. He had a chronic addiction to magic. He was terribly superstitious, invoking help from any 'magicians' who happened to be around. This person doesn't sound someone a holy book (the Qur'an) should call an exemplary pious leader, mh!?

Well it is true Cyrus II believed in the day of judgement – and that is what the Qur'an insists amongst others. And although Mazdaysm wasn't purely monotheistic, surely Cyrus and Persia's ruling nobles worshiped one great god 'Ahura Mazida'. Also (beware) he was very adopting that whenever he went he sacrificed to the leading deity of his subjects and told his admirers he worshipped their god. The first show of this was in Babylonia c.539BC. It immediately won him almost all the Babylonians when he worshipped and sacrificed to their Great Marduk – the patron deity of the city.

And Cyrus was so humble, very humble in his ways as the Qur'an rightly observes. He did this in life and in death. This is what, according to the Greek author Arrian of Nicomedia, Cyrus asks his grave visitors:

> *"O man, whoever thou art, from wheresoever thou comest, for I know you shall come, I am Cyrus, who founded the Persian Empire. Grudge me not, therefore, this little earth that covers my body".*

Still There Was 'The Fall'

Cyrus II had great ideas on ruling an empire. He lived those ideas and acted them well. Yet in his time the damn appetite for conquering didn't leave. He was attracted to continued warring, drama and subduing new lands – he only needed pretext to start it. He was a head of armies. That is how he acquired the epithet "lord of hosts' (overall head of armies). And because he also ruled over lesser kings (vassals/satraps) he was named 'king of kings'. That is, the king of those who are kings (the top of provincial/vassal kings).

Cyrus did informed reflections to find out what was wrong with empires. In his inquiry the conqueror discovered that he could press his 'subjects' only too much. The tighter the subjects' lives were made the riskier peace became. To soften the risks some false consciences he introduced include human, economic, legal and cultural rights.

The so called 'human rights' today were invented as response to practical needs of empire survival. They were thus meant for tricks. Some human rights we see today are 'psychological' outsmarting inherited from Persia. The Persians invented, though in rudimentary forms, the propaganda. And they somehow pioneered some blunt forms of psychological warfare. Those wars include ones that win the minds of subjects (e.g. cultural freedoms, secularism, material support and military protection) and those that convert enemies into allies (puppetry).

If one was careful to analyse the 'edicts of restoration' one would learn how they were meticulous war of minds (psychological wars). And the Jews succumbed.

It would take more than two hundred years for the subjects of Persia – Greeks ahead of all – to rise. After decades of external conquests and militarisation – while internal wrangling grew by the day – the empire became too powerful for outsiders yet weaker for itself. Weak, pompous leaders vied whilst an idealist population mushroomed. As should be expected, arrogance amongst the rulers had peaked. Times varied and the inside got wreaked in violence, terrorism and competition for powers. Sometimes usurpers readily took power, a mark of how fragile internal security had become. Darius III (381-330BC) for example would reclaim power on overthrowing a usurper. The empire had become internally weak because of clashing egos, too much knowing amongst the politicos and nobilities' mistrusted each other. Glories were waning. Alexander III of Macedonia saw (his generals actually did, not the boy king) that display of weaknesses and moved against Persia to take what they called a revenge. He defeated Darius III in a decisive battle at Gaugamela. Darius narrowly escaped Alexander's phalanxes only to be executed shortly by his own man – Bessos. That was the end of the great Persian Empire.

Why have I gone deep in the Persian civilization? Because therein are many socio-economic and political entries we take for granted today. Many people have no ideas we have inherited many parts of modern civilization from old Persians. I use them here as clear evidences of how far Achaemenes and later other dynasties of Persia had tried to build convincing subjugations (an empire with calculated manoeuvres). Their political state was so calculated and very aimed to fit its time, circumvent local deficits and meet temporal frustrations of humanity. The great Persian Empire assimilated all the spheres of the 'peripheries' lives' be they politics, military, technology, social structuration and religions. They adapted and immediately got too sophisticated than they had inherited from their subjects.

The future 'would-be-greats' of the earth e.g. Alexander III of Macedonia had lived exulting Persian nobleness. Again, Persia's subjects coveted-hated her (covet and hate psychology is real). This attests against possibility that one empire can outplay and outsmart others to place humanity in perpetual submission. I have gone deep into Persia to show that there is no way an empire can be so convincing (manipulative enough) to achieve the full 'Stockholm Syndrome' over her subjects. Those who argue America's hegemony is too sophisticated and smarter to end should think twice. America isn't yet half closer to what Persia was, not in the least...

The Root

Empires rise and fall, that is universally evident. Whether amongst the antiquities (such as Mesopotamians - Sumerians) or classical ones many were imperial powers that came and went. No single mass of people is so special as to rule all others forever. It can only be longer. However, greatness is but a fleeting moment. Even when they had the best of brains available put together, working and effective, empires came to pass. That way even when empires were quickly adaptive (as the foregoing discourse on Persia elucidates).

So, what is wrong with empires really? Is the answer to this question reflective of where America stands today? This author says yes. The root of empires' decline lies in the nature of 'humanity'. Humanity is evidently fallible and weak. It has marks all over it to make itself *repeatedly* wrong. Humanity hasn't left its animalism really. Mankind still live on the rules of nature. Not the rules of science. Least, the rules of logic. It is for this reason that at one time or the other men make mistakes that take them down. Murphy's Law takes its course and all there is, is an empire's downfall.

Murphy's Law;
Whatever can possibly go wrong, wrong it will go.

SECTION SIX: MAN IN HIS NATURE

Mankind Is Dangerous

It's naturally and humanly true that 'mankind is danger-ous' an organism. Man has been able to transform this once uninhabitable, wild earth into tamed natures. Not a mean feat. Mankind was able to do that because humanity is like no other species before. Man is 'danger' itself.

I have to start it this way as a means to summon you to re-think humanity, critically, and out of that connect to the rationale of the tell-tales of waning America. In the end one learns how connected the seeds of destruction are to the nature that mankind is endowed. Which is my way of saying Americans are following an exhausted path societies have had little to change.

That humanism is stubborn there is no question. That humanity does not despair even when it is facing 'endlessness' and 'darkness' is a legend common a knowledge. Humans face each dimension of life that comes their way emotionally, even when it actually wants mankind annihilated. The most enduring trait of humanism (human nature) is 'emotion' - it doesn't change just because humanity is piling a lot of knowledge. If you read Robert Greene's *"Laws of Human Nature"*, you have got to feel this dimension more vividly. How contradictory, mh!

With the certainty of violent ocean swashes and backwashes, human mind encounters every bit of adversities 'sadly or happily' – each at a time or simply mixed up. If need be, man does live in total pain and soon learn to enjoy it - creating what some call 'sweet pains'. Sadly, pain is known to strengthen mankind than happiness and sweetness can do. Because pain is real whereas happiness is an illusion. This is the most boggling anomaly you will ever learn in life.

The *psyche* of mankind resolutely encounters everything - whether good or bad! Mankind cannot be scared of anything - not in the long run. All throughout life, man has decidedly engaged with his troubles – mentally and physically. It underlines the concept of dualism – the twoness together. Mind alongside physique. The two in one body. With that, no crushing yoke has ever been able to scare her.

For human, vested in her mind and physique, there is a time for waning of everything. Everything is either coming or going - men observed this from a long time ago. Armed with this fact, men have since time immemorial learned not to 'depend on or fear' what is. Men have always looked forward. Classical philosophers: Heraclitus (c.535 – c. 475BC) and Empedocles (c.494 – c.434BC) called this fact 'state of flux'. They summed up that nothing lasts forever. The philosophers saw strife and love as natural. They saw change as a fact of life. Nothing lasts. Not even the gods. Not mankind. And if mankind cannot be forever, what about her own doings? The answer is so obvious.

So, we can be easy thinking of America's edifice. And within that thinking we are at advantage if we start accepting that the worst will unavoidably come. Sadly, for empires the end come too soon. Reading the present trends in the US socio-cultural dynamics, we should see there already are signs of imminent change. And they are necessary changes. Immutable changes that mankind visits on itself. And we see that those changes are springing from humanism, rather than America's material mightiness.

There is a time humanity hits 'itself' and all that it has goes down the drains... Material mightiness and superb skills (or intelligence) are no cure of that at all. Actually, as per history's own records 'the more advanced a civilisation is, the more likely it will die leaving little or none of itself when it is gone'

We see *now* there no longer is the USA born out of *brave*, pragmatic immigrants. All that remains is America born out of *softer* offspring. One that capitalises too much on Artificial Intelligence, lofty ideas and too much knowing. Knowing that is diverting from the logic of 'human intelligence' born of natural mind and pure physique.

The Root Of America's Decline

Humanism is our eternal nature. In academia humanism is labelled as a philosophy (an *ism*) contending for centrality of 'human reasoning' in everything mankind pursues. Many are insights in humanism but I am biased towards a few of them - those relevant to understand how America is losing her hegemony.

The foremost is humanism as 'a black hole' of contradictions. Herewith we find that humanity never rests in anything canvassing it. The human nature always gravitates towards controversy. It possesses an urge to do things differently. We tense not only when living in things set up through human arrangements but also in those brought by providence itself. Mankind never sits back humbled and waiting. This gives the answer to the question 'why Adam and Eve didn't simply bask in the Eden glories provided by their creator?' They tried the forbidden fruit. They dared try the wrath of their maker. So they destroyed instead of sustaining themselves. We still have that figment of self-seeking no matter what good comes our way. Yet our freedoms lead to ruin. All through history the ancients saw the sins that come from liberties and pleasures, and thus were always wary of freedoms. So they made laws. Not pleasurable ones, excruciating ones instead. Hence *Dura Lex, Cedi Lex* - harsh is the law but it is the law!

The ancient sages beheld that logic is contrary to our primordial nature. That is, our emotional and inquisitive nature. Because logic seeks to bring order and thus containment whereas the human nature seeks utter freedoms and wallowing in whatever it desires.

It is this dangerous contradiction of nature and reason we see in the US today. The more wealth, science, technology and wherewithal they are piling up the more inadequate, ineffective, immoral, loose, wayward and restless Americans are becoming (I had this discussed in details in several parts). Even with the America they dab the most developed democracy – with a very sophisticated legal practice – politicians still seek to tear each other apart. Self-seeking keeps clashing the logic of '*commonweal*' day in day out. Ego is increasing (taking the centre stage) its adversities much that people are stymied of what is becoming of their learned sovereignty. Politicians are thinking they know everything. That they are entitled to act whatever they like. And the citizens' hearts are pining away from immense voracity of politicians and weasel *mind* economists. Economists converting everything into economic assets and thus make everything go... see, legalisation of marijuana... economisation of sex dolls, trade in murders, liberalising the coital unions, staining the family sanctity, vending human sweat, public health, police departments, military skills, Intellect, Intelligence prowess, gun mercantilism etc.

Americans *now*, like citizens in preceding empires, cannot comprehend how with an enormous economy and massive technological production they still can have decrepit infrastructure. That they have a wobbling education and do live in an economic environment debt-ridden. According to statistics, every American is a debtor in this all that - from an ever present taxman to other irregular ramifications of policy category. This setup alone is a cause enough for decent men to miss fruits of freedom and pass sleepless nights no matter politicians outside there are advertising and passing laws for freedom and human rights.

Again, Americans are sharply prone to the *world* factors of economy. That is, many externalities have too much to do with their lives! This isn't the case amongst small, sheltered economies. Reluctantly, Americans have to reckon with the fact their lives are as unpredictable as was life amongst subsistence-based communities of the old. This is really nauseating. For it takes them back to realisation that their development, deciphered in its actual socio-politico-economic implications is degenerative. It keeps them on the beck and call of global trends - not free off. Trends that their Armies, politicians, economy, smart intelligence and any other element of power cannot guarantee. Because they are global, human, natural and all that. Their mighty sovereignty however clever that is must receive global trends as they occur. Hence the final consumer is certainly not well protected as many seem to believe. America's economy presents a very admirable façade (coveted) yes but in practice it is an angular grinding stone that presses each household in a unique way, at a unique angle. So they surely have 'our big economy' yet many have 'my meagre family income'. Because their big economy notwithstanding each household has to live by the *"ratrace"*. For those who care to investigate the setting therein represents the meaning of Ecclesiastes 1:1 – 20 'vanity of vanities, all is vanity...'

Does that picture ever allow personal freedoms, really? What about state of human rights? What about personal happiness? That is enough whataboutism. No wonder the US has never featured amongst 'toppers' in the list of the happiest people (happiness index) in the world. They cannot be. Think it careful.

Fact has it in air that no matter how much the US gathers through foreign extortions, sacrifices of her boys in endless wars, scheming through puppets, arm-twisting her allies (the modern days' satraps) and manipulating her spheres of influence, the empire cannot get enough. She remains the leading global debtor (a state borrower). So it was in empires gone. No empire ever had enough.

Surveys of world civilizations made by this author can suggest the reason empires struggle this much. I have it intoned in most parts of this book wherein I present on the role, position and impact of the US Army and Intelligence Agencies. It is that empires eventually stretch out THINLY through their occupational Armies. But in practice the Armies are complexes that consume chunks of resources. This means Armies carry with them a significant value of liabilities. Yet the stretching cannot stop once imperialism is in motion. It continues until troops are ineffectually spread *although* they still continue to be adept at outmanoeuvring their 'home state'. This whilst in practice what they do outside is no longer profitable! People back home *then* panic because they have an economy so large, many boys dying elsewhere in soldiery - in far off lands - and powers phenomenal *yet* they are in an economy very uncertain. Nothing to them ever is enough. The vanity (for citizens who can see it) becomes disquieting. Citizens toiling day and night *now* feel duped of their status and worthiness. It is time for reckoning...

Humanism rush in. And the centre cannot hold...

Overlooked In The Art Of Empire Building

Humanism is a shoddy rubric that all changes spring from. Overlooked in the art of empire building is that citizens do not live things or arrangements. The people are not to be taken for granted. Humans struggle for changes whether the shifts will build or destroy them in the long run.

Americans, like citizens of empires before them, dream changes no matter their government's bellicose policies are bringing dollars or not. Currently for example, they are openly distasting the fact that their Armies and spy agencies are scourging outsiders for wealth, richness that when brought in is *naught*. For it gets caught by the hands of a few (corporate societies). They see that their boys are fighting, making wars that for *a large part* have only accelerated global migrations to the West. A very sad development. They are often heard articulating that the Washington establishment and the upper, richer classes are taking them for a ride. The same way they evolved and decided to say "no" to "black slavery" although it still was profitable, Americans are no longer willing to sit silently seeing what their military is doing outside. It is a step forward, very big one. There is nothing the US government can do to stem that growing outlook either.

Mankind is known to possess that faculty. The ability to understand things and take a stand, for or against. It is a matter of time. It will be a short while before the 'warring culture' either stops dead or risks turning out outrageously infamous. Then thereabouts a dilemma is going to unfold. That is, in the foreseeable future foreign wars will be playing an electoral card. This time against each seating government. The trickiest part of it all is this; America's wars cannot be stopped especially because this empire is a hegemony of military intelligence. Minus warring, this empire is stuck in limbo. Remember Jimmy Carter's admission? 'The USA is the most war-like nation in the history of the world'. If she ever stops warring, off she will be gone.

For humans, it is always like that. Power takes *soon* to control the rulers. Insatiableness is forever at the heart's bottom of power wielders. Muammar Gadhafi, the ex-President of Libya tried some charms to coax the people. He wanted to sustain his insatiableness. He gave his people free foods. He created farms in the desert for them. The Bedouin President helped finance his people's conjugal processes in the traditions of Arabian excesses! The man provided free schooling and a universal health service. He thought the citizens would leave him alone. He thought they would fuck real hard and lie down calmly, full of lethargy. May be he thought without being hungry citizens relax and slumber their lives. He thought with all those Libyans would leave him alone 'to ride the state office' forever. Well, he was wrong. That isn't a page in humanism. The citizens took few decades before they pushed him down the cliff. He is gone, gone in a barbaric way.

Humanism pushes on until there is change whatever the direction. In the case of Libya we are witnesses that the direction of the push was towards poverty, misery and hopelessness. It was degenerative. As we see Libyans kill each other like wild beasts, we cannot help it but wonder the follies of man. Yet, that is the average man for you.

As American politicians (read: Plato's democratic man) push to liberalize everything, introduce serious novelties and alter the core values that made the US great, America is living humanism. We (watchers) are in for a spectacle, of a clash – a war between reason and sensibilities. War of the legends: emotions versus logic. Human nature against knowledge.

It isn't a trifle.

Recently, for example, the US government in its sanctimonious audacity resolved to make homosexuality legal. They drew a lot of logical lines. They poured rhetoric about humans, nature and the foundations of rights to that end. The Congress and Senate resolved that science is right. They celebrated reason. The President assented some laws. Reason prevailed, so it seemed. But what? That was the President, Senate and Congress. Not the people. For subsequent to that the people of USA voted in a new President who had *openly* promised to crush the setup and work to restore America's family values (including the tested and proven roles of a good dad and a good mum).

Researchers would later show that religious people, amongst other factors, were overwhelmingly responsible for the Donald Trump win. The devout had remained silent throughout *gay* legalisation processes. They had avoided polling their views but they moved when what seemed an opportune moment sprang up. That is how smart sensibilities are. And that is human nature. People can go along anything even when it is so abhorrent to them - they can lie quiet and wait. Patience it is. In short, through the Trump vote, the people spoke that they doubt the academics. If that wasn't enough a speech, surely they will speak again – *obviously* louder. For that is how mankind expresses his conviction... In the same vein, Americans are sleeping on a lot of frustrations that will one day surface to surprise the power players.

The worst of the foregoing, as far as the US society is concerned is this: America is at a point in time an imperial power transform into something disquieting e.g. a nation with a perceived global citizenship. People in this society espouse reduced patriotism and embrace doubt of over-defensive nationalism. Why? Because their state (her practice of imperial grandeur) happen to have already taught them the love and beauty of internationalism and thinking globally. In the next part I expound on what socio-internationalization leads into.

History says 'societal internationalism' is not something to fall in bed with, if one can help it.

There 'Has Been'

State arrogance is part and parcel of mature humanism – the US politicians are playing it well. Like the way the elites amongst dead empires degenerated into arrogant, personality wars: in Babylonia, Persia, Macedonia, Greece, Rome, Mongolia etc. We are witnessing America's powerful classes outdoing each other over trivia. Self-centredness and *clientela* (ancient Rome's political legacy based on patronage) are manifest through 'Tea Parties' and the 'Deep States'. There are other clandestine arrangements *specific* to the nature of the US economy. None can simply know all the tricks there are. Those are arrangements caused by political selfishness, arrogance and ego. The US politicians can conceal their dealings. That much they can. But Political historians unmistakably know that many backroom scheming do backfire. It is a no brainer. There comes a time schemers vie, win, draw and lose - fortunes always come in twosome (good or ill).

For the first time in the history of USA there is a dully, democratically elected President (Donald John Trump) to whom majority politicians say is an impostor, a disgrace – that he was not elected and does not deserve to... This is another kind of USA, one not known before. A petty USA. Obviously there is an arrangement backfiring somewhere in the backrooms.

A loser of popular votes isn't new. There has been. Woodrow Wilson lost hugely in 1913 but the people and politicians still were sane. Today, they aren't sane enough to stand for the laws. But it is the law. It flabbergasted them. They ran heaven and earth trying to unseat him. Ever since Trump was elected, the state is partially crippled and is working half-mast. Going on in the backrooms is some kind of 'political' vendetta. The establishment is virtually blaming everything on Russia, on Trump and on Heaven. Election is no longer the usual times full of voters' theatrics, no. Why? They say Russia is interfering this or that. Heaven knows Russia is twenty folds weaker Intelligence wise.

What is real is that the US politicos now doubt their own elections, their electoral system and the people. Soon they will doubt everything. And at last doubt themselves. After all, the growing culture of fake news, misinformation and prevalence of psy – ops are already digging deep in their beds of knowledge, eroding the degrees of trust Americans may have had of their political system. When they eventually realise they have no credible 'informants' to trust any more, why won't they doubt themselves?

It is a matter of time.

History knows better. That the aforesaid kind of *self-defeating* leagues will continue. Such leagues are known diseases of civility communicable faster at the end of each imperial era. Majority of those diseases are now clear before our eyes... They are going to graduate into a socio-economic goblin eating the US political establishment. Plato had it right. Clashes of ego will keep growing in Washington until the greatness they worship is wholly consumed in an internal race of acquisitiveness, self-assertiveness and surmounting personal ambitions.

In history, divisive figures keen on self-assertiveness: Artaxerxes II of Persia, Alexander III of Macedonia, Julius Caesar and Augustus Octavian of old Rome etc. were epitomes of the winding imperial powers.

It is a hundred years since the US started out as an actual hegemony (review part two and three of this treatise). At the age of one hundred years old (the ancients called it a hundred full cycles) all supremacies (all great things as well) start weakening. It is the bravery of nature that says so. Woodrow's brainchild cannot be exceptional...

The Last Throes

Shall the throes that will squeeze last air from America's imperial nostrils come from outside? The answer is simple, 'a yes-no', but in it largely a 'no'. The outside is going to contribute resoundingly but the opus lies inside. I repeat this the fifth time: Empires die from within.

Even as you read this, America continues destroying herself at a pace faster than outsiders can ever cause. I have made a run for the nature of destructions being heaped upon her in all sections of this treatise. This concluding section hasn't been exceptional. I say, externalities, however evident they seem, are statistically minimal and supplementary. It is in the records that for an empire to decline troubles must start within, not without. Otherwise, any disturbances remain *tempestuous* and come to pass.

For the true power of an entity is in its internal strength. And any successful change must, first thing therefore, herald from there. It is simple to understand, simple to overlook though. It has proven evidences.

History of empires indicate that when internal progresses exceed the carrying capacity of the core population and thus empires go out to snatch resources, create prestige and retain the means to stand tall amongst nations, they earn – amongst others – new mind-sets that destabilize the inside (e.g. manipulating their own people). It goes back to Newtonian "actions and reactions are equal though opposite". When the outside states (allies and puppets) burn and there is no place left to hide *goyim* (people of the nations) either fight or submit to imperial fangs. Submitting or fighting, this is what history says. President George W. Bush passed that highway of history when he called out 'you are either with us or against us'. He in effect refuted the rights of neutrals. This was in the wake of 9/11, 2001. His judgment was predictable to those who know 'the life and times of empires'. Full imperialism knows no neutrality. A thing that is scary in effect.

The US is thereabouts. Submit or fight. She has scourged the outsiders with many attempts at controlling the earth, such that all that remains of 'sovereignties other' – in Latin America, Asia and Africa – has become submitting to the US and Co. i.e. the Western powers. A hundred plus global leaders today are puppets, allies or doormats of the United States of America. Where anything contrary to this exists fire is burning or economies are melting down. This there have been/are politicians who have had more to tell. Amongst them the late Slobodan Milosevic, Hugo Chavez and one can *now* ask Nikolas Maduro of Venezuela.

And where fire is burning humanism is playing its last card. In many regions, people have submitted to US manoeuvring. For example in Iraq, Libya, Palestine, Somalia, Afghanistan, DR Congo, the Central African Republic, Southern Sudan and others people simply stay put. Somehow the people have taken pains to heart and allowed it to inure them. But that doesn't mean they cease to think. They have humanism as their ally – the nature that reasons. In many 'burning' countries people are adopting what 'humans' naturally do and have been doing over the ages of human history – taking to their heels. Moving on, that is. Today the world has neutral words for the move, 'looking for greener pastures' they say, for example. Yet it is what it was, 'running away from negation'.

Where fire isn't burning but the US imperialism is chorusing louder people are, likewise, playing humanism. In 'Spanish America', Mainland Africa, Eastern Europe, Asia and the galaxy of islands dotting global oceans people have humanism to save their skins. How is this humanism being played? Read on...

Come To America, Come To Europe

It has all along been like this. When might become right –
the decider – the weak territories get emptied of their people.
Wreaked in insecurity and mounting desperations, utter negation and abysmal poverty the lands have their people escape
troubles by trekking far off and away. Today homes in Asia,
Africa, Eastern Europe and Latin America are getting deserted
as young people run away to the West. They are walking away
from lingering poverty, uncertainty, diseases and insecurity (in
short: negation). A simple yet humanly solution. It is too hu-
manistic. Basic. It is deduced from an assumption that 'Western
powers shall bomb everywhere, badly trade goyim but will always show mercy to Westerners. Because charity begins home'.
The emigrants seem to be fettered to an idea that 'let us flock
there, there will come a lasting peace'.

The ongoing emigration to the West, as it is today, is a sort of
dispersal mechanism. The young generations of the third world
are choosing to westernise instead of dying unattended like
their parents.

Social psychologists are concealing this grand picture and reports from aid agencies, humanitarian NGOs and social think-
tanks are deliberately overlooking this scary picture. The fact
is: defeated by abject poverty, stingy unemployment, excruciating social dismissal and their leaders' lack of *common* senses
and responsibilities, the third world youth is throwing hands
up and 'willing it to the devil'. They are migrating through
nightmares. Global oceans are now dotted (days and nights)
with thousands illegally migrating sons and daughters of *les
miserables* from poor countries. Those youth share one dream,
a dream of better life abroad – one impossible at home. It's
the American Dream. The American Dream is now the world's
dream. A good reason we can no longer have the usual earth
there used to be - not with the world now getting full of wealth
addicts.

The paupers of the earth concluded sometimes ago that rather than staying and dying on empty bellies to be home; trekking hundreds of miles, ferrying across choppy seas or catching the 'birds of the skies' to airports in America and Europe might make sense in the end. Whatever the detours they are taking, however long they will take yet their final destination - in the end - is the USA. The concept of 'green pasture' is a concept of a better place. Many youth are dreaming of USA as their choosy destination because it is the greenest. The American Dream. The US alone was receiving around 50,000 immigrants a week (as per a 2018 US statistics). Projections in the same book indicate the trend was expected to soar. And that some migrants were repeated movers who had used Europe as transit - with their eyes on the US in the end! So, this migration is phenomenal in a way. It is all en route to the US. In all considerations this is an alarming development. The walls they are building in USA are a reaction to this alarm. But it is bound to fail. It is absurd really. For even through legal migrations, a lot of youth in many countries can still afford it. They still can saturate the US of A. And there are graduates all over the world who, after a long time of *educated unemployment*, are being convinced by their families, relatives and friends to take their certificates and go try for a job in USA. One can only guess how many the US is going to take on before her people are out of jobs themselves.

Well, the West is suffering from the mistakes it has been doing for centuries – that of piling a lot of wealth in their 'Metropoles' while disabling the rest. Migrants are simply being reasonable.

Greatness Has Great Prices

That is the impact of 'the American Dream'– and the bloodhound 'Make America Great'. Greatness has great pays greatly paid. If no new nation(s) democratically and economically fertile rises to 'aid' the USA acting primary destination of global migrants – in the immediate present – there will be no 'great

USA' by 2070. The land, the economy and the people will have metamorphosed into 'a global sort of community' with fuller competitions for identity, wealth and power. I profess for the rise of '*ethnicism*' that will be in force to propel 'acceptance versus rejection' in jobs, initiatives, investments and social services. The problems of 'humanism' we see in the West today, combined with millions of ambitious immigrants, variations of socio-cultural orientations, reduced racial perception and scary material dreams will have quadrupled, thus, triggering social DISLOCATIONS.

One Time In Egypt

You need precedence of social dislocations, perhaps? Well. Almost all dead empires had this social evolution (dislocations) in their heydays. No matter how pretty romanticized that is. Here I can only illustrate an example. In the 19th part I treated a bit about this as far as Old Persia is concerned. I indicated that at one time, Ecbatana, Persepolis, Pasargadae, Susa, Babylonia etc. filled to the overflowing. To this day the people who live in the wide area have a 'shock' of an unprecedented mixture that speaks a volume of great gathering. Let me now single out the ancient Egyptian Kingdoms for more clarification.

The Ancient Egyptian kingdoms: the Old, Middle and Late Kingdoms died *mainly* of social dislocations. The old kingdom survived around 2573 – 2150BC, Middle Kingdom survived around 1970 – 1645BC whereas the Late Kingdom lasted 1550 – 1350BC. They were at one time conquerors to the south (Africa) and north (Asia) making themselves greenest of pastures. In those times, the empires were unequalled in the wider geography. Outsiders reckoned with the fact that Egypt was well ahead. They immigrated mostly to lower Nile and modern Alexandria. Well known groups of newcomers were the Hyksos and desert tribes from the south of Arabia. The Jews had flocked in as multitudes, totally abandoning their hunger stricken patches in the desert of Sin. This, one can use the Tanach to read.

They were running from hunger and poverty – the sons of Jacob.

The newcomers from the Middle East, Arabia, Kush and Europe imported their cultures and legends. Their learning and superstitions. Their families and social theories. The Egyptians were at this time the most tolerant people on earth! One could drag in his dog-worshipping-faith. One could bring in the ancient moon god Nanna. And the question of equality and human rights were fully granted such that the citizens of foreign descent at one time had their 'local communities ruling themselves' in their cultures, their faiths and their laws. Interesting, uh! The immigrants would abuse the native Egyptians for worshipping Pharaohs amongst the gods. Egyptians eventually grew ashamed of their ruler – a mortal god (the same way the USA is growing ashamed of Christ). That was a serious mistake because a divine pharaoh had been at the core of Egyptian society, identity, unity and citizenship. One couldn't just throw away Pharaoh and still have an Egypt well intact.

One can ponder on this history and learn a lot reading, especially, the Egyptian Middle Kingdom – the eleventh, twelfth and thirteenth dynasties are collegiate. Egyptologists know well what sprang out of excessive immigrations... They agree yes the mix made Egypt a global place yet restive as well – newcomers eroded the land's core values and at last tore her apart. It would take Kamose, a pharaoh of the seventeenth dynasty, to see that the problem was the 'independent immigrants' not the gods. He moved against the Hyksos (now full citizens and enjoying strong political powers), subdued their autonomous polities and reunified the whole country. Then the second intermediate period of Egypt was ushered in. This period eventually restored the mighty Egypt now as the Late Egyptian Kingdom.

At this point, I must make myself clean on the theme of migration and immigrants. I have conscience and I am aware it is an issue so delicate, arguable and complex. But the path I have taken in writing this book denies me some freedoms of convenience. On all issues I am, firstly, taking a realist path - writing everything as right as it is known to historians; not 'interpretivist' economists. I see my reviewers, some of them being Asian immigrants to America and Canada, had had prolonged arguments. Heated as should be. Good arguments *for* migration. I am happy at last we agreed to honour knowledge and accept challenges. The issues I just submitted about Egypt they agree are factually true. And the best thing is one can unearth similar scenarios in almost all gone hegemonies. No sociologist refutes mass migration is *mostly* destructive of societies. It only spins arguments when the capitalists and economists come in with their bigger than life projections and theories.

An added example: the Middle Eastern Christians immigrating to Rome in the first century AD would in a matter of few centuries totally destroy the Roman culture (esp. making the great pantheon laughable).This affected the Roman society and superstructure. It transformed Rome's social philosophy, the energy of personal agency and belief about destiny. With all that metamorphosis, Rome was hasten to decline...

The hegemony the USA and Western Europe created seem to be headed the same way. They made that well known error frequently committed by the leading powers. One that involves building pre-eminent economies capable of co-opting others and swallowing them. Having other economies in their bellies, the US and European economies in effect, become the bellies of the earth! It is what I see with the changing global humanity. The West is a society foremost built on the Christian philosophy, morality, unity, cohesion and interpretation of life. Whether they have worked on this core or prepared it for massive societal changes now imminent is any one's guess.

In section one, I show that gathering all the global wealth to the West effectively made the countries a global emporium. Thus America and Western Europe have become that legendary fruitful tree everyone has to throw stones onto to strike a juicy one. They have become centres of global successes, failures, inconsistencies, hope, dreams, tussling, immorality and you mention the rest. They can only take too much.

Power Enterprises Are Dethroned By Weak, Innocent Civilities

A thing noted throughout history is that powerful hegemonies are rarely languished. I mean no alternative powers ever rise and conquer them easily. They die a natural death. A demise involving internal rivalry and slowly self-invalidating, self-strangling and eventually stagnation. Now, this is when another power can push an empire down the cliff. In the same vein I don't see China or Russia beat the USA. Neither the populous India nor anyone else. I see excessive love of honour, economic arrogance and extreme love of freedoms, destructive human rights and the eroding family ways lying to waste the might USA.

There is nothing so special about the USA that is unassailable either. Neither her people nor her geography is. All one sees is the USA was built by a no nonsense, uncompromising, persevering and conservative lot of family men and women – the parents who recognised and identified family ways as critical to their survival, identity, labour and self-propagation. The US family unit had been the launching pad of strength and self-mortification – preventing children from getting spoiled by what they saw or daydreamed. Hate or love the USA but give credits to her forefathers' rightful recognition that the family is so special and priceless.

But 'the US family' is *now* under attack and disregard. It is molested that we are soon going to see two cohabiting men or women for that matter, allowed to adopt children and call them a family. The *sanctum* of a family is being destroyed... that and all its functionaries. Hence, fulfilment of William B. Yeats'

> *'The ceremony of innocence is drowned;*
> *The best lack all conviction, while the worst*
> *Are full of passionate intensity'*

In 'Down the line model', Collin Renfrew presents a progression of culture in a trickle down sequence, from the centre towards the periphery. I find the model very useful for explaining what is going on in the USA and the world. I have to make a go for it. I interpolate some minor changes to the model though.

Lord Renfrew's '*down the line model*' is basically that of a diffusion wherein cultural traits (he was using obsidian dispersions through that founding study) are spread down the line from the core (origin) through points of destinations. Say the core is A. And from A spreads B, C, D ... (capitals being countries, smalls being localities in those countries). According to the model, the influence of superior cultural assemblage from A down the rest will be felt in trickling (decreasing) order. That says, the influence of A (now call it America – USA) will be well felt at point B (now call it Britain) but will decrease more at C (now call it Costa Rica). That goes on decreasing further down the line at D (call it Democratic Republic of Congo) and so on. At points u, v, w, x, y and z (these being localities within a country) the influence of A (USA) is much reduced and almost nil. Herein lies the complexity of civilizations.

It Is Not Safe To Be Alone

The complexity of civilizations is what the USA is grappling with. One that is causing her to push hard to make sure other countries immediately adapt to her laws, culture, world views, scientific trends and social outlooks. For she knows *if* sluggishness at adapting to her changing society persists in other countries, the USA will soon be well ahead in cultural and behavioural trends (in a wayward manner) that her people will seem way outlandish. This speaks a volume. Amongst them that humanity is too connected than is apart.

The US isn't dishing out billions of dollars for her loved human rights, gender movements, gay rights and others to be spread world over because she so loves the earth. No. The USA is leading the world towards her ways because she knows she is self-destroying and crossing the lines she shouldn't. She cannot help it really. She has to drag others on.

Some examples of that cabal mission you can easily prove. If an American comes to Africa today and is asked to explain how children 'neo-liberally' and 'rightly so' deserve to abandon their old parents to paid care houses, to die in the hands of strangers working for money, he/she suddenly gets ashamed. She can't solidly hold ground. Or, if a pair of American gay couple roams a street in Dar es Salaam hand in hand, surely that becomes a stunning abomination to the residents. And the two will certainly end their day in discomfort. The reason being that people there cannot find proper explanations for 'a man' playing 'a man' and another 'playing a woman'. The residents there have any number of girls to play that end. Women in Dar es Salaam are possessive of their sexual tradition. They are the first to pick on a man subtly showing the first signs of homosexuality attraction. No such couple can live comfortably before their eyes.

Again explaining endless legal divorces and partners getting married the third time or more is laughable to many. This not only amongst third world countries. I have a German friend in Berlin, a professor in anthropology, who have had classes in which (he reveals) students heatedly wrangle on the divorce matter. They don't find supportive reasons a single person should be a suitor or bride for the whole of one's lifetime. And that is in Berlin, see? Some things are simply unexplainable. Laws allow it or not, if you had to attend your mother's (or father's) second, third, fourth, fifth or more wedding receptions - time after time - you would run insane. The Berlin students seem to have discussed the issue along that line.

Well the reason the USA is very vocal about some human rights, even trying to push them down the throats of other nations, is that she is afraid she is going way outside the normal line. She is creating a society, hailing from the impact of the economy, which can only share little with the world. Their sense of freedom is slowly diverting from the ordinary. And it isn't safe to be alone. She must carry the rest with her down that way of self-destruction.

Yet the 'trickle down model' above means there will always be people (somewhere) who preserve their traditional civilities, humilities and faiths (in the eyes of core Americans those are weak, immature civilities). In a world that the core (the USA) erodes rapidly and the ceremony of innocence drowns, the peripheries grow 'affectionable'. And even convincing. Soft-powers, that is. This explains why a number of core citizens in USA is increasingly intermarrying foreigners in a wave that is suspicious. Many of them (girls and boys) are facilitating pecuniary logistics for migration and naturalisation of their lovers. Is the US aware of this development? She is, I presume.

I ask because I have run up and down to find literatures on this trend but come up with little written. What I am using here is primary data from connections, church experiences amongst pastors and individuals narrating what they know. They say boys and girls are using their hard earned funds to make sure they bring in lovers from afar. If one promises to love and last, one has a girl (or boy) thirsting for this. Because she wouldn't want *a repeat* of all she saw between her 'equality-minded' father and mother! See? Others are converting *en masse* to foreign faiths – looking for solace. They are looking for the old, innocent religious civilities. A good chunk is gradually espousing pure foreign cultures and honour. I argue in part eleven that this is a tale of longing. Suspecting Americans have started longing for eroding sets of values. The core values that are waning in their dear USA. They are already looking for them where they still are or, at least, they are looking for a semblance of what they used to be.

As of new immigrants (recent US citizens), they are mostly bringing in their values e.g. beliefs, conviction, commitment and focus. When it is time to marry, many are turning back to look for partners back home and then fly them in. Some are even teaching this Abrahamic tradition to their offspring born in the West. That their sons and daughters should go back to some remote villages they never lived in to ask for a hand in marriage. For those I asked the answer was almost uniform, "you marry someone there when (if) you want endless violence in your house or imminent threat of divorces every short while.

They are too independent. They no longer accept marriage as a burden and a sacrifice. The people there believe in their *rights*". Well I couldn't put in a word because I have had that more than I am willing to seek.

A Bank Of Stubbornness

Humanism doesn't rest in chagrin or happiness – it is not as preposterous as 'patriotism' is. It extracts more energy towards endless ends – mainly acquisitiveness, inquisitiveness, identity formation and attempts to achieve superiority. Humanism is a bank of stubbornness. And this is what fails empires. Yet it is what makes us real humans. The story of how humanism makes us who we are (as individuals and as societies) goes back to some dialectical philosophies on thesis, antithesis and synthesis... But this parable is way not for this treatise.

This work isn't an extract from a PhD or any other honorary paper to that end. It isn't professorial either. It is an analytical *reflection* by a humble analyst, tutor and commentator. This author happens to be a historian (sp. archaeology) who for once benefited immensely from studies in ancient histories. The knowledge of ancient empires, civilizations, colonisations, man and his environment, evolution of states, social formations and ensuing power dynamics studied by this author are responsible for building most arguments contained herein.

This monograph is written with deliberate simplicities to avoid being thrown away as 'academic' and is entirely for public consumption. A public that has recently evolved from being a strictly academic (read: scholarly) readership to an easy, internet addicted audience. Thus this work is written with acknowledgement that the traditional form of non-fiction writing that is stilted, slow and boring can no longer be a communicative success. One needs to tell facts in a simplified, casual and *fast-paced* manner that people can feel attracted to. Revealing contradictions, follies, analogies and anomalous issues became a tactical choice. Thought provoking became unavoidable.

This author confesses having written this work with an eye on experimenting new, possible forms of writing *facts* – what if I choose to write truths in a casual, storytelling - conversational manner? Assume I write a teacher to learner essays that are not *strictly* standard essays? Well, this author was thinking thereabouts.

The aim of this release is to mark out, through simplified texts, instances present in the US imperial guard that when learned from 'old empires' are proven to have been causes of 'crashes' of civilizations and eventually downfall of empires.

The thesis herein doesn't call for battle of arguments but heats the readers' nerves to encourage exploring, reviewing, reconsidering and reflecting on what is going on within the US imperialism – keen eyes on comparison with what happened amongst empires gone. This author suggests that the A, B, C, D … for majority empires' downfall have remained more or less the same across centuries of civilizations. And concludes that the reason is 'we have remained humans over those ages'. A people's hegemony, however magnificent it becomes, does have limitations.

All issues treated therein are arguable as should be any topic of this nature, focus, impetus, form, direction and magnitude. Yet nothing is without evidences either in this very simplified text or out there in the world the US plays her charms. In fact they are issues one can explore and easily catch-up with in the news, global annals of events, political/military diplomacies, technological inventions, social façades, books and the effects of the US policies. A host of academic literature is out there waiting for ones willing to review. They need little to no efforts. This author is working on following suit this version with an academic version for libraries and those who still need intellectually written books i.e. one containing: full citations, footnotes and bibliographies – it is coming at the heels of this.

America is surely *listing* and her problems come from within the power itself. Then, they go out to the world where America keeps arm-twisting nations for eminence. Eventually retreating, her *scheming* haunt her from within – *now* in full force. All there is, is déjà vu. They happened times on, times off in the history of civilizations.